The
**Lonely
Stories**

ALSO EDITED BY NATALIE EVE GARRETT

Eat Joy:
Stories & Comfort Food from 31 Celebrated Writers

The Artists' and Writers' Cookbook:
A Collection of Stories with Recipes

The
Lonely
Stories

22 Celebrated Writers on the
Joys & Struggles of Being Alone

EDITED BY
NATALIE EVE GARRETT

CATAPULT

NEW YORK

ISBN: 978-1-94822-660-8

Cover design by Jaya Miceli
Book design by Wah-Ming Chang

Library of Congress Control Number: 2021944225

Catapult
New York, NY
books.catapult.co

Printed in the United States of America
3 5 7 9 10 8 6 4 2

For Tony, Serafina, and Aurelio

Contents

Introduction

What if we joined our sorrows, I'm saying. I'm saying:
What if that is joy?

—ROSS GAY, *The Book of Delights*

While working on this book, I held that quote in my mind, but with a twist: What if we joined our loneliness? What if *that* is joy?

With *The Lonely Stories*, I hoped to summon cathartic personal essays illuminating the experience of being alone—stories of our solitude and stories of our loneliness. Because although talking about loneliness often seems taboo, even a source of shame, we all feel it sometimes: when we're adrift in a new and unfamiliar place; while searching for a partner or feeling disconnected in a relationship; in the isolating experience of being misunderstood, undervalued, or disrespected; when seeking kindred spirits and community; when navigating online and in-person experiences; and during passages of life including heartbreak, illness, and grief. Joyful stories of aloneness were also welcome, because even though we all experience the sting of loneliness, so often we feel replenished by solitude.

I wanted *The Lonely Stories* to offer readers a range of entry points, with essays touching on topics including aloneness and gender, sexuality, addiction, immigration, insecurity, and illness—achingly relatable essays, regardless of life experience. More women than men responded to my invitation, so this book encompasses more of their perspectives. Our society tends to expect women to hold everything and everyone together, socially and emotionally; women who relish being alone are the witches, the misfits. So it felt right to make more room for women to examine and honor the shape of their aloneness.

The book began before the pandemic. While much of it was written during the long days of quarantine—private memories of aloneness, poignantly drafted during our collective aloneness—the majority of the essays reflect not on the pandemic but on earlier times. For me, in the wake of living through such an intense period of isolation, the premise of the book resonates even more strongly, and the healing it offers feels even more necessary.

While putting together *The Lonely Stories*, I was drawn to essays about the quiet delights of solitude and the shocks of isolation, as well as reflections on the gentler waves of loneliness that come and go throughout our lives. I longed to create a harbor for our most vulnerable stories, told with urgency and sometimes with levity—affirming stories that might reassure and reconnect us. Most of all, I hoped to shine light on a universal emotion and experience that is often pushed down into the dark.

Throughout my life, I've experienced the pain of loneliness, yet I've also come to cherish solitude. When I was growing up, I used to imagine that all of the past versions of me were still everywhere I'd ever been. It was a bit like believing in ghosts and a bit like having imaginary friends, but they were just younger versions of me. I'd spend an afternoon romping through the woods alone; at night, lying in bed, I'd picture myself out there, eyes shining in the dark. Part of me genuinely believed that I was still out there, or that day's version of me was, and that all the other versions of me that had ever romped in the woods were out there, too. As an introspective, creative, and also frequently sick kid, I found this vision both slightly unsettling and profoundly reassuring: no matter what happened, I'd always be there for myself.

Episodes of prescribed solitude were a constant throughout my childhood, precipitated by chronic sinus infections, undiagnosed migraines, waves of unrecognized anxiety, chronic fatigue before it had a name. In my elementary school class, I was the one who was "always sick," although I felt ashamed when classmates would say, "You're *always* sick," as if to suggest that I was never really sick but instead secretly wanted to spend days home alone in bed, my hands pressed against my temples and around my eyes, pushing back to counter the stabs of pain within. Overall, I was fortunate: my afflictions were neither severe nor life threatening; I had two caring parents with good health insurance; my mom could afford to take time off of work to shuttle me to dozens of doctors and help me recover from two regrettable sinus surgeries. Nevertheless, there was no magic cure. Sometimes the only way out is through.

So I waited it out, in the dark, alone. When my head throbbed, there was nothing to do but lie in bed and rest; noise and light just made it worse. My imaginativeness was in part a product of all of this alone time, but it was also a balm for it: it was hard to be deeply lonely when surrounded by the hazy echoes of my former selves.

Now in my forties, with children of my own, I still get those migraines—in fact, they come with greater frequency. Reclusive recuperation, though, is harder to come by. Instead, I often find two sweet children jumping on me as I lie on the sofa with a compress over my eyes: "Do you need a hug, Mommy?" In times like these, when I'm struggling to hold on, I sometimes find myself flung back to memories of my children's even-younger selves—the downy ringlets and squeakier voices, the way my daughter said *pleps* instead of *please* and my son hoisted himself upright by hugging my leg. Every once in a while, I catch a glimpse of my former self in them, too, or spot a shadow of myself out the window, scrambling over fallen trees in the woods, calling me back to me. These glimpses of the girl I once was, and in a sense, still am—wide-eyed, fragile, unsure, and brave—make me feel less lonely. Every once in a while, I just need that reminder: I'm still here.

The desire to hold on to fleeting feelings and experiences is part of what propelled me toward my love of painting and writing and, ultimately, toward the dream of conjuring this book. And while loneliness can be devastating, I find it deeply moving that it can also function as a portal to beauty and discovery.

In *The Lonely Stories: 22 Celebrated Writers on the Joys & Struggles of Being Alone*, Imani Perry confronts chronic illness, while Aja Gabel offers a meditation on miscarriage and hope. Jean Kwok grapples with the particular loneliness of being an immigrant, twice. Jeffery Renard Allen delves into his childhood fear of losing his mother, a single mom raising him on the South Side of Chicago. Jhumpa Lahiri reveals the ways in which books have offered consolation in lonely times. Anthony Doerr shares his comedic struggles with internet addiction. Lidia Yuknavitch sensuously revels in solitude.

The writers in *The Lonely Stories* are at turns tentatively dipping into solitude, struggling not to sink into isolation, and enriched by self-discovery. By sharing their heartfelt stories, we're reminded that we're not alone in feeling alone. Maybe that helps alleviate some of our loneliness; maybe it reminds us to handle our aloneness with tenderness.

If you're feeling lonely or if you've ever felt unseen, if you're emboldened by solitude or secretly longing for it: welcome.

—NATALIE EVE GARRETT

The
Lonely
Stories

Brief Important Moments Where I Was the Only Person on Earth

MEGAN GIDDINGS

The Only Person in All of Mid-Michigan

The bus was supposed to arrive every morning at 6:20. Depending on the other kids on the route, depending on deer, depending on cows, depending on the snow, depending on the melt, it could be 6:10, it could be 6:30. My family's house was a quarter mile from the road and if I wanted to walk slowly and not feel rushed and grumpy, I would have to leave the house every morning by 6:00.

Our driveway was unpaved and unlit. I would walk in the dark listening to the world around me. Songbirds anticipating the sunrise. The snuffs and snorts of deer in the woods on the left side. Wild turkeys making their arguments in the soybean field that ran along the road. Cars starting up. My breathing. The clomp of my boots when the dirt was dry. The crunch of them when it snowed. All of these things were important because these walks were the only time of day where I was completely alone.

I shared a bedroom with my younger sister and with my older sister whenever she came home from college. Our house was large but arranged in a way where the only places I could be truly alone were in the tub, taking long baths that led to my mother complaining to me about the propane bill; in the basement, where I would pull out my Rollerblades and skate for hours in circles, circumambulating the same pillar as if that would somehow lead to enlightenment; or outside, on our lawn, reading. There were six of us, and my parents sometimes talked about how quiet things were in our home, because they had both been raised in small houses with at least nine other siblings. Whenever they spoke about their childhoods, most of their stories were about "we," their rat-king-esque collective memories between them and my aunts and uncles. The space of our house felt like luxury to them.

Walking alone in the driveway, standing by myself waiting for the bus, these were the times where I could become certain about things. I would consider my opinions. I would think about what I liked and hated. I would write in my head. Constantly being around other people, their emotions, their opinions, their knowledge, made me feel engulfed in them and simultaneously aware of how little I understood myself; I craved that time alone.

My friends at school would sometimes ask me, "Aren't you afraid of being alone in the dark for that long?" And the tone of their voices, the way they asked me, made me think I was childish or fooling myself. "Some psycho could drive past and just abduct you. By the time people realized you were gone, you would probably be dead." During those conversations, I would feel flooded with their fears.

When I tried to talk about my own specific fears and frustrations, I could always feel the distance between us. My friends, like the average rural white person, rarely had to consider how their race influenced their relationship to the world around them and themselves. Sometimes, I would complain about how it felt like everywhere I went, Somewhat-Well-Meaning and Not-At-All-Well-Meaning Adults were constantly bringing up the fact that I was Black. Teachers at school would say things that made it clear they worried that if I slightly wavered, I would be pregnant, or a drug addict, or waste all my potential. Nothing they said about being Black sounded anything like the life I was living. So many days felt like white adults were trying to make me a side character in the movie of their lives. If they could just get through to me, I could be their *Music of the Heart–Blind Side–Freedom Writers* kid.

My friends' faces would turn elsewhere. Suddenly every French fry on the table would have significant importance. Why bring that up when we could talk about why K. and L. were no longer friends? Why talk about something musty like shadows on snow, when we could talk about who got caught hooking up in the school elevator? What do you mean you don't know who you are? Eat this Little Debbie and stop being so weird. Stop talking about being alone. It makes you sound sad.

The Only Person in the Movie Theater

Sometimes, women younger than me ask me for advice. I think it's partly because I'm tall and an occasional professor, but mostly it's because I have the stink of older sister all over me. There are people who can smell the spiciness of judgment, the green scent of empathy, the bottom vanilla notes of tell-me-what-you-really-want seeping out my skin. Before 2020, I would tell younger women—especially those who wanted to be writers—to go to the movies alone.

The friend I was supposed to go with bailed because the drag king she was flirting with had finally responded to her texts. The house I was living in was old and overfilled with people, and we were all broke and fighting about when we could turn on the air conditioner. So I bought myself a salad, slid it into my tote bag, and went to the worst theater downtown. Its chairs were tortuously uncomfortable. Despite being on the second story of a building, the theater lobby's carpet smelled like cigarettes, butter, and basements. Inside, the air was too cold, the movie was bad but had terrific clothes, and somehow, I was alone on a Wednesday night. I sat in the back and tried not to chew my lettuce too loudly. During the credits, I turned instinctively to the empty seat next to me. I was embarrassed when I realized that it was the first movie I had ever seen alone.

There are so many good reasons for women to not want to be alone in public. Even during the day, in that fairly safe college town, there were always people shouting racist things at me out of car windows, men trying to talk at me, people assuming that because I was in public, I was open to and ready for an uncomfortable conversation. All the men I was friends with at that time regularly went to the movies alone. They'd tell me about the blockbusters, the art houses, the classic movies that they had seen. Out with my boyfriend or other friends, I would see them, men walking around alone at night, smoking cigarettes, oblivious to everything but nicotine, wind, and the shape of the smoke drifting out of their large mouths. I wanted that freedom.

It feels almost cliché now to write about Virginia Woolf's *A Room of One's Own* when considering necessary loneliness and creativity. But I've always admired when other writers are frank about how money is truly a necessary factor when it comes to having the space to make things. I tell women to go to the movies alone because there's something I think contemporary women need at the beginning of their art lives maybe almost as much as money: that feeling of freedom, where you don't have to consider other people or their needs, or the ability to cultivate a barometer of self-reliance that can come from even something as small as going to a theater by yourself, seeing something, and not feeling the urge to tilt your head and gauge the amount of fun other people are having.

So often, women are conditioned to be people pleasers. To be the ones who keep things smooth and pleasant for everyone around them. I tell women to do these things for themselves because worrying so much about other people can smother the risk-taking part of your brain that writing needs. It's a small thing. But in the dark theater, I learned that I didn't need to look at someone else's face lit by a screen to understand how to feel. My emotions are valid. Sometimes I can simply look into myself to know the world around me.

The Only Person in the Cold Lake

A certain kind of person is always surprised when I talk about loving kayaking or swimming. Some of them are blunt about the root of their surprise: "I didn't know Black people liked swimming." It's been one of the few truths about me I've known since I was young. Swim classes since before I even had a sense of memories. In a pool, the only thoughts I had room to have were about my body. Kicking my legs, releasing breaths, gauging my distance from the wall, flipping, and back again. In high school, I took a swimming survival day course. You jump into the pool and practice treading water. You learn how to take off your jeans and potentially use them as a flotation device. The instructor talks to you seriously about cold water shock and what happens to your body in low temperatures. You're told that survival is about the skills you learn, but it is also about mind-set. Stay calm; never think, *Oh shit, I'm dying*; make quick, calculated choices. This is all to explain part of why I was kayaking on a lake on a cold, gusty October day in southern Indiana. I was not afraid.

How many times in my life have I ever been able to accurately say, "I was not afraid"? There are times where my anxiety is so out of control that my heart starts pounding from the house settling. In the winters, a vast murder of crows will gather in the large tree in my side yard. I'll be in bed, afraid, and have to remind myself that the sound I hear is only birds. Spiders. Mice. What if I step on a nail? It'll be lodged in my foot. I read the news, I'm afraid. The sudden adrenaline surge when I see a Confederate flag on someone's car. Sometimes, I think of my anxiety as one of those pictures that you look at one way and it's a vase. Squint or move your head around in some way, and it's two faces looking at each other. Am I anxious because of brain chemistry? Or is it because the longer I've been alive, the more and more I've understood that the United States can be a deeply malicious place to Black women? When you're a Black woman here, you can be asleep in your bed and people will still find a way to blame you for being murdered.

I talk about the picture because I know it's both. There is the irrational mental health part and there is the rational, which comes from enough threats, enough othering to make you feel like you regularly have to be ready for all the miserable possibilities. Canoeing, kayaking, swimming, all of them help when I am too much brain, too many feelings.

On that October day out on the lake, I watched geese flying overhead and thought about what it would be like to know you must always be leaving to live. The sky was clear, the only sound paddles dipping in and out of water. A fish flipped and made a perfect splash. The wind was gusting at forty miles per hour, and I stayed as close as I could to the sides of the lake. Then, during one significant wind burst, I misjudged how to shift my weight, and my kayak capsized. In a flash, my body was in the air, and the wind was a great beautiful howl. I plunged into the water. For a brief moment of terror, I was stuck under the kayak in frigid water, before I pushed the boat aside and surfaced.

One of my feet remained caught in seaweed. My husband, kayaking nearby, paddled over to me. "You have to calm down," I said, or we'll both go in. Each of my thoughts was at most six words long. I was not cold or tired. There were others, paddling farther out in the lake. I called briefly for help, but no one heard me. I knew the cold would hit me when I lost the initial adrenaline rush. A man on the shore about three-quarters of a mile away waved at me but did not seem to understand I was in the water. I knew I was wasting time.

I kicked and pulled and just when I thought I would have to extract my foot and leave my shoe behind, it loosened. I told my husband I would swim to shore. He should meet me at the boat rental and tell the people there I had capsized. I swam and tried to keep my mouth as closed as possible. The water stank. Rot, dead leaves. I could not turn around and look at my husband. My hands guided me. When I could touch the bottom, I stood up, walked. On the side of the lake I came up to, there were two ways to reach a trail that would guide me back to where I started: climb up about eight feet or go back into the water and swim for maybe five more minutes. Slowly, in my soaked clothes, I pulled myself up, touching tree roots, feeling it out, gritting my teeth, letting my fingers press into the rock and soil. When I was up into the woods, I let out a breath. My brain came crashing into my body.

I took off the soaked life vest. I lay back into some weeds and breathed. Somehow that moment felt more perilous than anything I had gone through to be there. I felt certain that my heart was going to stop from the mixture of cold and adrenaline and suppressed fear. My breath felt too hot. Eyes burned. Later, I would take a shower until the water ran cold. I would wash my hair, I would scrub myself with a loofah and lose myself in the heat, the steam, the ersatz coconut smell of my soap. Even later, I would take this experience and write it into a short story. When it was on the page, I would notice all the ways I bent the experience to make it entertaining, to make it fit the story, and feel a little sour. In the woods, I was briefly sure I would take one last breath, close my eyes, and that would be the end. I tried only to observe, not to think or feel.

The wind blew again. Aureate leaves left their trees and gave the air shape. The path was clear and well-marked. No one was in sight. *You can do anything now*, my brain said, and for once, I didn't disagree. My entire life, I've had to remind myself how precious I am to myself. That I deserve to be taken care of, that it is worthwhile for me to be alive, that I am not taking up space. I took off my sweatshirt and tried to wring it out. Alone and cold and wet, every tree felt like a blessing.

If other people had been around, I would've felt the need to reassure them that I'm fine. I might've had a more emotional reaction. When we found each other, my husband put his big, warm hand on my cheek and said he had never been more scared in his entire life. We cried together, our heads on each other's shoulders. But in the woods watching the leaves, trying to get dry, I had never been more myself. *I can do anything*, I said. My voice was calm. Clouds rolled in. I picked myself up and began to walk.

Javelinas

CLAIRE DEDERER

I'd been told I would be fetched at the El Paso airport by a representative from the foundation, and there he was, near the baggage claim, a white-haired cowboyish person who introduced himself as Douglas. We got into his car and made our way to the freeway and then along the Rio Grande—"There's Ciudad Juárez," he told me, pointing across the river—and after about fifty miles we hung a left, away from the river and into a landscape of complete and utter brownness. As we drove, I chattered away, trying to convert him to a pro-Claire stance. When I look back at this period, I marvel at how much time I spent trying to make people like me. Trying somehow to *convince them of me.*

Finally, three hours after we'd gotten in the car, we were in Marfa, circling its lazy streets, and then I was alone in my little adobe house. True aloneness was a rarity for me—a wife, a mother, a person crowded all the time, it seemed, by other people.

I unpacked my suitcase first thing. I folded my T-shirts and underwear into drawers, hung my hopeful dresses in the closet, lined up my clogs and sneakers by the front door, stacked my books on the desk, spilled my pens into a mug. When everything was put away, I sat on the hard, red leather couch like a patient in a waiting room.

The house was silent for a minute and then loud with the noise of teenagers going by on their way home from the high school down the street—laughing and shoving each other. I'd left my teenage son at home and I liked hearing their rough, silly voices. Once they'd passed, silence fell again.

I had been given, out of the blue, a residency fellowship in Marfa, and here I was. I would be living entirely alone for a month and a half in this little house filled with good art, modern furniture, and walls of books by writers who'd come here before me; the names on the spines left me dizzy with unworthiness. From my window, I looked across town to the Chinati Mountains, dry and low and gentle, unlike the looming wet hulks of the mountains of the Pacific Northwest. Back at home, even the landscape was crowded—furred with trees and personal history. Here I saw emptiness.

Into the emptiness came a familiar, insistent thought: something was wrong with me. This wasn't a new thought. It was a thought I'd been having for years, or decades. I shook it off as I'd taught myself to do. Mothers can't sit around thinking shit like that. I picked up my backpack and walked down the street and across the train tracks to Porter's Market, which Douglas had pointed out on our way into town.

Porter's was a little down at the heels: the floor's linoleum tiles peeled up at the edges; the vegetables were either wan or too bright. I could buy only as much as I was able to carry home in my backpack. I picked out apples, bread, milk, coffee, eggs, butter, and a chocolate bar and made my way back to the beer and wine area. I bought two bottles of what looked like an okay Malbec. Paying, I was riven by self-consciousness. I was used to shopping for my family—my daughter was away at college but I still had my husband and teenage son to take care of. It was as weird as a cactus to be buying just a few groceries for myself.

As I walked home, the sky took on a soft periwinkle color. The bottles clanked in my backpack. I made scrambled eggs and toast and—sitting in the dining room with its shelves of books by past residents David Foster Wallace and Colson Whitehead and Deborah Eisenberg—ate my modest dinner and drank one of the bottles of wine while I watched *The Great British Baking Show*. Finally I fell into bed.

At 1:00 a.m., a train rolled through town and woke me up. For several seconds I had no idea where I was.

Over coffee the next morning I dutifully made my way through the binder you always find at residencies: what to do, what not to do. The first page of the binder was a sheet with this headline: "Javelina, NOT Just A Nuisance Animal!"

The fact sheet explained that javelinas look like pigs but are in fact a kind of peccary. The javelina's signature stench is produced by a dorsal scent gland, which the fact sheet assured me was "easily taken care of," an alarming phrase. I learned that javelinas roam ranchland and sometimes towns. They gather in family groups of five to fifteen; their vision is so poor that when they try to get away from a perceived threat, they often don't know which way to go. They'll charge if provoked, not out of hostility but out of sheer dopey confusion. The fact sheet, with its repeated assertions that the javelina was NOT our natural enemy, was clearly a piece of propaganda, designed to defend the javelina against its detractors. The document's friendly tone—"So what do you say we learn a little more about the javelina?"—did not fool me. What it described was a nightmare: gangs of smelly, hairy not-pigs roaming the streets.

By the time I finished reading, I counted myself firmly among the javelina's natural enemies. But it didn't matter because I planned never, ever to meet one. I would avoid all run-ins with potentially dangerous adversaries.

Drink coffee, write, go for a walk, go to the grocery store, make dinner, drink wine, fall asleep. My days were simple, and small in scope. The foundation had provided me with a car, which I left in the carport, sensing I was better off on foot—less likely to get in trouble.

Every day I circumnavigated the town. I felt most comfortable where the houses stopped and the scrubland started— on the streets in the middle of town I was confronted with people living their normal lives and felt my aloneness more keenly. I walked along the edge of the ranch near my house, up the small hill above the MARFA water tower, past the house with the Wu-Tang mural, and over to the Chinati Foundation.

Chinati was the institution that made Marfa an unlikely art hub. This had been an ordinary bit of nowhere back in the 1970s, when the sculptor Donald Judd bought the decommissioned army base on the edge of town and moved his life and consequently the art world to West Texas. In the wake of Judd's death, the Chinati Foundation oversaw the army buildings, which were now devoted to his work and the work of his famous friends. I skirted the foundation's walls, though, focused on my walk, undistracted by art.

Halfway through my walk each day I stopped at the Get Go store for a grapefruit Jarritos and a soulful gaze at the butch cashier, who was about my age but appeared to be free of my burdens: children, husband, book contract, hair.

Each day I went into the study and produced a thousand words, but there was something wrong with them, because there was something wrong with me.

Sitting at the table with David Foster Wallace hovering over my shoulder, I read my own tarot, trying to find out what it was—the wrong thing. But the deck kept throwing up the same card: the Devil. In the Universal Rider Waite Tarot, the most commonly used deck, the devil is depicted as a hairy-legged man-beast, with a properly satanic upside-down pentagram hovering over his head. The Devil is the card of circular thought, of enslavement, of addiction.

I was good at interpreting the tarot. When I read for friends, I spun wild abstractions and unnerving conclusions from the cards, which gave themselves up to this kind of abstruse interpretation. Everything meant something else. Friends loved this magic trick, the way I could manufacture meaning as if I were a meaning-making machine. Yet I felt stymied by this appearance of the Devil. I re-threw the spread and got the Devil again. And again. What are the odds, in a seventy-eight-card deck? Why did it keep coming up?

Staring at the Devil card, I decided I was addicted to negative thoughts and self-hatred. *Self-hatred*, I thought to myself, pouring another glass of wine.

Given the amount of time I spent walking the town's perimeter, it was inevitable that it would happen. Finally I saw a javelina in person, as it were—up by the Chinati Foundation as I churned out my miles under the midday sun. I was just passing a large installation by the artist Robert Irwin when I spotted it crossing the road. A furry horizontal rectangle: a huge head and a barrel-shaped body atop four spindly legs. It looked like an especially vigilant member of a homeowners' association patrolling the neighborhood—relaxed yet thuggish. It *owned* this corner.

There was no way I was following it down the street. It might have a buddy or twelve waiting down in the ravine ready to jump me. I turned around and headed home the long way.

•

I walked an increasing number of miles per day. I was flagellating myself, circling the town like an anchorite. At the time I
thought I was practicing good health. At the time I didn't see
I was seeking ways to manipulate my body, and the hours my
body moved through, as a way to prevent myself from looking
at the chaos.

Each day I resisted going to the liquor store. Each day I
told myself I would not buy brown liquor, only wine. Then
I would walk down to Porter's to pick up another bottle of
Malbec. Porter's became a site of drama. I wondered if any of
the nice, chatty cashiers noticed my daily purchase. When I
bought my bottle, I always bought ingredients for a healthy
meal too, and always I made myself a full dinner, even if I
mostly ended up pushing it around on my plate.

Another image: not flagellating myself, but a screw, rotating
around and around, going farther down with every turn.

Aloneness was a posture I was adopting, a crouch I was drop-
ping into. I stopped calling my husband. When I finally did
call him after an unconscionable number of days, he said, "I
guess you're turning into a lonely cowboy poet. I hope you're
happy." What neither of us said: I'd been alone for years.

Pouring glass after glass of wine is the most alone thing you can do. My life was full to the brim, and yet in the midst of it, I just wanted to be left alone with my bottle of Malbec.

A lonely cowboy poet. It didn't sound so terrible to me. I wanted to be someone different, someone who had nothing. That sounded like freedom.

A year after my time in Marfa, my husband and I read a news story about a woman in a suburb north of Seattle who died of exposure in her front yard during a snowstorm. She was found under a bush just a few yards from the house. My husband wondered, *How could this have happened?* But I knew exactly how it could happen. It was easy to imagine wandering out of my house, wanting only to get away from everyone so I could be drunk in peace.

Once I'd seen the first one, I began to see them everywhere. Sometimes out of the corner of my eye, I'd catch a scuttling movement on a quiet street end, a hairy rump disappearing behind a shrub.

Outside my house grew a luxuriant prickly-pear cactus. When I examined it closely, I saw that its spiky paddles had cartoonish bites taken out of them—bite marks just the size of a javelina's mouth.

.

One beautiful, balmy night, I furtively looked up the liquor store hours on Google and climbed into the dreaded car. I drove under high, starry skies down San Antonio Street, past the Dairy Queen, past Porter's, to Celebration Liquor. I entered nervously, knowing I was stepping into dangerous territory. It's not that I had never drunk bourbon before. I'd drunk literal gallons of bourbon in my life. It was just that I'd never drunk bourbon in a house where I was going to be alone for days and weeks. I knew what would happen: The bottle would start to glow at me from the cupboard. It would glow until its light was the only thing I could see in the house.

The guy working the register was what my friends and I have always called a hesher: a white rocker dude who emanated lowlife vibes. I vibrated with shame as I set my bourbon on the counter and paid the hesher, with his knit cap and his tattoos. How could I convince him I was respectable? I wanted to tell him about the walks, the healthy dinners, all the writing I was getting done.

I stopped throwing the tarot because it just kept giving me the same stupid Devil. I began to walk even farther. I broke off from my regular loop and walked out on the state route into the scrubland, as far as I could, and then I turned around and walked back into town. I came to see that the landscape wasn't so brown after all. The greens were not insistent like the greens of the Pacific Northwest, but they were there, a soft sage on the hillsides. Even the dirt wasn't brown but a luminous rust color.

I was worried that this was all I would take home from Marfa. I worried I would do no meaningful writing. I worried I would make no serious friendships. All I would have to show for my time here was an impression, a memory, of color. I would remember the changing light of the sky, moving from silver to lilac to a hard, unforgiving blue.

A gang of javelinas liked to hang out at the slightly dilapidated playground down the street. They glanced over with interest when I passed; I sped up and hoped they wouldn't spring one of their ill-conceived, pointless attacks on me. I looked up some javelina videos—apparently they ran amok on the streets of Tucson. I felt an atavistic terror when I saw one; they seemed positively satanic to me. But in Tucson, they were considered mere suburban blight. Not such a big deal.

Javelinas—not a big deal for the citizens of Tucson, Arizona. Why did the small deals all feel like big deals to me?

The javelinas seemed to be coming nearer to my house. I thought I smelled something musky and rotten from my bedroom window. I wrote jokingly to a friend that if she didn't hear from me again, it would be because a javelina had come to my door, swooped me up, and carried me away, *Officer and a Gentleman*–style.

•

Getting ready to leave on my morning walk, I oh-so-casually pulled a single card from the deck. The Devil. Are you kidding me? I threw it down and slammed out of the house.

One thing about living alone is you become painfully aware of the number of bottles in your recycling. I drank all those? The bourbon was gone so fast!

A week before I was slated to leave town, there was a must-show party at the Chinati Foundation—the kind of party people dream of going to, something like a thousand bucks a plate, curators coming from all over the world. As a writer-in-residence, I was invited—indeed, expected—to attend. I pulled one of the hopeful dresses from the closet and just before sunset I drove up to Chinati, parking just a few yards from where I'd seen that first javelina.

The party was in one of the decommissioned army buildings, and the high, light space seemed filled with everything good in the world. The party was like a giant beating wing, rising and falling; you could feel its movement when you entered the room. I ate beautiful food that looked like a tiny garden on my plate. I drank a special cocktail with a special name. I met a poet and a photographer and a musician and a museum director. Chairs were moved in fits of enthusiasm as people jumped from conversation to conversation. Intelligence and money and glamour, three entities that too rarely meet, shimmered together over the room, almost gaseous, a cream-and-silver-and-pink aurora borealis. In the middle of it, even as I chatted and smiled, I felt utterly alone. My arm moved like an automaton's, lifting glass to mouth.

I drank as if we were all having an experience together, but really the party was just an interregnum in the trajectory I'd started in my solitary glass at home—a trajectory that would end with me passed out in bed.

I drove home drunk, in case you're wondering who's the villain of this piece. I sat on my front porch, drinking bourbon, breathing in the freedom of being alone in the night. I had endured the party and its glitter and its brilliance like mortifications, though I'd worn the pretty dress and I'd never stopped smiling. All evening, I had wanted only this: a private envelope of close, dark air; plenty to drink; no one to talk to. I heard snuffling, or maybe I was imagining it. Was I smelling something? I thought maybe I was smelling something. I hung over the side of the porch, trailing a hand, listening for javelinas, wanting them to come for me.

Did the devil make me drink eleventy hundred bottles of wine and bourbon and miss the entire experience of being in Marfa, the entire experience of *being alive* for the past however many years?

If so, what entity was it that visited me the next morning, as I lay grainy-eyed in bed? For suddenly—and it truly was sudden—knowledge inhabited me: the knowledge that my drinking and my misery were one and the same. For the first time, I admitted to myself that I hadn't missed a day of drinking in over ten years—ten years when my personal misery index skyrocketed. For the first time, I admitted to myself that I had binged and blacked out and driven drunk and lied. In short, I'd done all the things drunks do. In the empty desert morning, suddenly it was as obvious as a dumb joke.

What was it, I ask you, that made me fix myself a cup of coffee, sit down in the Eames chair by the window, open the computer, and google the words *alcoholism test*?

I groggily, warily clicked my way through something called the Alcohol Use Disorders Quiz. I didn't answer all the questions honestly, but I revealed a little of how it had been for me. The test spat out my answer: I was exhibiting "harmful drinking behavior."

I thought to myself, *Hm, I wonder what would happen if I told the truth.* I could at the very least experiment with the truth. I took a deep breath and restarted the test. When the results came back this time, it was news I already knew somewhere inside me.

I stretched out on the living room floor with the high desert sunlight streaming all over me, and the decision to stop drinking happened to me. It was the saddest decision in the world—the decision to stop being alone in that particular way.

•

The following week, Douglas came to drive me back to the airport in El Paso. I had not had a drink in seven days. As we drove away from the little house, I leaned my forehead against the window, watching the neighborhood slip past. Down at the playground, there were probably a few javelinas, hanging around like extra-smelly teenage delinquents. If they attacked you, it wasn't because they were angry. They were just confused, like the rest of us.

Ward

IMANI PERRY

They enter every few hours. Some are nurses, others cleaning staff, rarely interns, residents, or even physicians. The bags of fluids, narcotics, and antibiotics each have their own feeling. Your body sucks them in. At least that is how it feels. Maybe it is better described as an infiltration. They seep in. Uninvited, invited, necessary, excessive. The ache of the needle is consistent. Some dreams masked as reveries, monster-filled and memory-filled, are scared away by workers. You cannot get a good night's sleep there.

A hospital room gives loneliness its peak expression. Introverted, in my daily life I frequently extol the virtue of solitude. In a house of books, with a lot of memories, one's dead and fantastic companions come and go at will. A feast, a tea party, or a tête-à-tête, it's your decision. But in the hospital, these gatherings of solitude slip out of my grasp. The comfort of alone is absent. The floor, naked, gleams clean. It reflects nothing. Smallness expands like a funhouse.

Beyond the closed door you can hear bustles that are none

of your business. On the other side, people work and chat. Snatches of melancholy laughter and personal travails are never loud enough for you to eavesdrop. They take breaks, they transport people. They are tired. They work. The lights that turn everyone sallow are on. They rush to quell crises. The crisis here, inside, is no one's urgency.

I wasn't in this time for complications from systemic lupus or Graves' disease. The last time, this is what happened: I had three kidney stones. They lodged inside somewhere and caused an infection. This was good: The pain brought me into the emergency room. And in the process of examining me, doctors and nurses noted that I was experiencing a thyroid storm. A thyroid storm is "a life-threatening health condition that is associated with untreated or undertreated hyperthyroidism. During thyroid storm, an individual's heart rate, blood pressure, and body temperature can soar to dangerously high levels. Without prompt, aggressive treatment, thyroid storm is often fatal."*

I also had sepsis, from the infection. It entered my blood. "Sepsis is a potentially life-threatening condition caused by the body's response to an infection. The body normally releases chemicals into the bloodstream to fight an infection. Sepsis occurs when the body's response to these chemicals is

---

* Kristeen Moore, "Thyroid Storm," Healthline, updated September 28, 2018, www.healthline.com/health/thyroid-storm.

out of balance, triggering changes that can damage multiple organ systems."[*]

The quotations from medical websites are a safeguard. In my own words, when I tell people, friends, these things, they move past them quickly. It is not that their discomfort bothers me. It is that I don't know if they turn their heads to the right from discomfort only or also from disregard. Not of me, necessarily, but of truth.

The last time I was in the hospital, someone forgot to give me toiletries for the first two days and nights I slept there. Someone has that task. Someone is more likely to remember if they see that the patient is someone's worry, if a person comes with the patient and, in nervous declaration, asks questions, is solicitous, maybe even aggressive. I was alone and slept over eighteen hours each day. The paper underwear grew sour with sweat. I felt a pauper's grief each time my eyes opened. So I closed them again. Later I would say, "I didn't ask someone for toiletries because, you know, I was so disoriented. But I would think they would just do that as a matter of course." Matter of fact. In retrospect, it was more likely depression, not disorientation. The swirling sort.

Fabric is gentler than paper. I wanted to be held close in fabric. I tried to remind myself of what could be worse. Well, a catheter certainly. The worst part of the catheter is that the discomfort is greater than the humiliation. How low are you when

---

[*] "Sepsis," Mayo Clinic, www.mayoclinic.org/diseases-conditions/sepsis /symptoms-causes/syc-20351214.

you stop caring about someone tending to your siphoned waste because your energy resides in the worrying pressure on your ureter, a part of your body you are accustomed to not knowing at all, no matter how much you use it? Yes, that would be worse.

You beat back the day's sorrow with cleanliness. I remembered that wisdom the third day. Section and braid your hair into plaits. Brush your teeth thoroughly. Wash, wash, and wash. Spread the watery lotion over you. Tie on the gown with care, as though it is clothing. Stuff the old gown, the old pants, the old sheets in the corner. Even, hunched over in hurt, smooth the new ones on the bed. Stand up for a while. You feel better if only for exactly how long it takes to realize that no one sees or cares about your ritual, least of all you.

The television is nakedly honest in a hospital room. It does not suck you into its fantasies. It is a cacophonous box, boring and squawking. You turn it off. You turn it on. Both ways it's annoying. How is it that it cannot be comforting here, where you most need comfort?

This time I did not eat, because the deprivation felt like another act of cleanliness. Only ice chips and sips of cranberry juice. A few crackers. This peculiarly religious, and especially Catholic, behavior creeps up on me. The redemption that I think I'm making is foolish. This has never been the kind of thing that brings other people closer. It does not offer you a shoulder to cry on or a hug. What are you trying to redeem?

Outside I am different. Highly competent. I manage work and life. *I am building a legacy*, I think, in the most hubris-filled moments. There is always the nagging worry of being like Ivan

Ilyich, however. Ilyich, from Leo Tolstoy's *The Death of Ivan Ilyich*, is the kind of bourgeois person who, in addition to having misguided priorities (I don't think I have those, or I don't want to think I have those) lives in the delusion of an endless life—of ever-blooming competence despite daily frustrations—until he learns he is going to die. We are all going to die. But for Ilyich, death is coming soon. First it was small. A fall, an injured side. It persists. It gnaws at him. The doctor looks for a cause. There is no remediation. And life slows to a halt in anticipation of its end. "And he has to live like this on the edge of destruction, alone," Tolstoy writes, "with nobody at all to understand or pity him."

I haven't ever received a terminal diagnosis. It would be easy, therefore, to refuse the way Ilyich stays on my mind. But my thoughts keep returning to him. Because he learns this lesson: there is no virtue that prevents the body from failing. Not absolutely. We can be "healthy" in deed, and indeed, but even at our heartiest, we are most frail.

I was not going to die—*soon*. That's what I learned when I was first diagnosed with a chronic disease twenty-four years ago. But I was going to live with the immediacy of my body's potential failure at all times. The thing they say to me—"You could have died"—when the illnesses flame always alarms. "The infection that made its way into your bloodstream could have spread. You were nearly too late." Sometimes they say, "If it had been a few more hours." Sometimes I overhear them, tutting at me, judging my failure. I wonder if they think the ill lose their hearing. There is a veil between us, between sickness and health. I am a ghost in those moments, without perception, a task. "Sepsis," they whisper. "She didn't report feeling pain earlier." The students try to shine when it happens at the teaching hospitals. They are smug in their assessments, eager to point out the perceptual deficiencies of the patient. I wonder how many of them have spent a day teaching, writing, cooking multiple meals, driving one hundred miles, checking homework, managing what feels unmanageable. How many of them shine so brightly before they burn and tumble.

Ilyich grows impatient with the people in his life, who do not want to talk about his impending fate. The emotional scampering away is common in sickness and in death. And the vacancy of my hospital room is a reminder. A funhouse of refracted and repeated loneliness. There are, of course, people who, after the crisis has been averted, say to me, "Why don't you ever, why didn't you ask for help?"

The implication of the irritated question is that asking to the point of begging has not been a feature of my life for years. But, I have learned, people usually don't want you to ask. People want you to be satisfied with what they have to give and to never say another word. *Generosity* should honestly be split into two words, one for the giving to another, and one for the giving that is a self-congratulation fitting neatly into how the giver sees himself, regardless of the other. The latter is in abundance. The former? Oh, it is rare! It rents the veil too much.

After he passes, the lesson of the death of Ivan Ilyich is even more potent. He is gone; there is a funeral. His colleagues feel grateful that it was not them. They are eager to do the memorial in a quick and perfunctory way. Show up, pay respects, follow ritual. *Yes*, I think. *We are so afraid of death*. So much so that even disease and disability are treated in this way. People delight in not being afflicted like you. It is an ugly human trait and I am afraid most of us have it. The moment I am free and clear of the hospital, it slips into me, that ugliness, for all the lonely people still on the wards. Ashamed, I know this is a terror that bars necessary intimacy. Courage is in short supply when it comes to these matters—except in the moments of great love. Perhaps that is the purpose of love. It isn't just the warm feeling, the joy. It is the prospect of a human integrity beyond what seems possible.

My son was brought by his father on the fifth day. He asked if he could get in the bed with me. I scooted over to make room. He said, "I just didn't know, I've never been in the hospital before." Oh, how I loved that. The honesty alongside the desire for closeness. I am so glad my teeth are clean. I am so glad the mustiness is off my body and I am well rested enough to smile honestly at him. We are noisy when the woman who works in food service arrives. She smiles at him. "Handsome boy," she says. He is lithe and vivid. When she leaves, we turn our noses up at the food. I eat the crackers and drink the juice. I do not sleep as long that night, but my rest is not fretful.

•

In *The Death of Ivan Ilyich*, it is his servant, Gerasim, who soothes
Ilyich when his spoiled family fails. Gerasim, the peasant,
knows the true meaning of life and the inevitability of death.
He is tender and attentive. It is one of those vexing portraits. It
is true, the bourgeois often worry about the wrong things; poor
folks are often closer to understanding virtue and decency. But
it is also a romantic projection, and here, as in place after place,
this portrayal deprives the peasant of the interiority of his own
struggles and suffering. He exists mainly as a lesson. Literature,
even great literature, is full of this. But there are in fact people
in this world who maintain the gift of clarity when it comes to
kindnesses. Children have it, usually, but we socialize them out
of it. At some point they learn that a tearful reaction to bleed-
ing is not okay. Lying down when one's stomach or heart hurts
is vanity. Working in ways that strip your soul is applauded.
In children, we replicate ourselves in the worst ways. Thank
goodness they hold on for as long as they can.

I have always been afraid of colonizing my children's lives.
Of relying on them too much. You have children to let them
go eventually, hoping they will stay connected to you, but
you are not entitled to that. Emotional responsibility should
not be a bullying thing. It should be a loving, intimate thing.
It should be a sewn-together thing. But I would be lying if I
denied that it's the sunlight of a child breaking through the
loneliness that saves me every time. It will not decimate it. It
will just ease it when nothing else does. This is living.

Mother-Wit

JEFFERY RENARD ALLEN

He saw his train speeding toward its spanking-new counter-part, a game of chicken, although he knew the other train could not move out of his path. Released the high guttural horn in warning. Nowhere to run. Nothing he could do other than listen to the friction of the brakes and rhythmic, stopgap clanging of wheels against rails and wait. On impact, his older, sturdier-built engine tunneled through the newer model, sound of metal tearing through metal, structure reduced, steel veering away in long lines. The second train a calabash spilling out commuters, both the living and the dead. In the aftermath the air was left shaking. Sound dwindled. A weighing silence.

For a hairbreadth I'm caught in the wreckage, until I manage to follow the calligraphic lines of the rails through the clanging swirl, pull myself free, and take on flesh again. Lurched away, all still in the room save for the sound of the television, a modest-sized black-and-white model, a few years still before my mother and I would own our first color console. Thinking back, in the root of my mind I see the television set, a hollow bulky box with faux wood paneling, gray images

splashing inside and gurgling sound. Almost fifty years have
passed, yet I still can hear the news anchor's voice reaching me
as if from underwater, another dimension. I was experiencing
the realization of my greatest fear as a child, that my mother
would die, leaving me all alone.

My mother often commuted on this train, the I.C. (Illinois
Central), to the Loop on weekday mornings, then transferred
to a second train for Winnetka, the northern suburb where she
made thirty-five dollars a day working as a maid—"daywork,"
she and her friends called it—for a wealthy white family. That
morning—October 30, 1972—she'd readied herself as usual
to the rhythms of easy listening sliding out from a small radio
we kept on the kitchen table. At 7:00 sharp she'd left through
the back (kitchen) door, a morning like any other. I'd pro-
ceeded to bathe, dress, cook breakfast, before sitting down on
the living room couch with my overflowing plate of food to
watch *Ray Rayner and His Friends*, speed-eating and drinking
through my meal: glasses of milk and orange juice, four slices
of well-buttered toast, two eggs over easy, and four strips of
bacon, covered by a collapsed tent of maple syrup. I was ten
years old, tall and skinny for my age, although I had a vora-
cious appetite.

A special news bulletin brought my morning to a standstill.
At the news, I put my plate aside and remained seated on the
couch, mulling over my options. My mother usually arrived at
work around 9:00, so rather than leave for school, I decided to
remain at home and call her employers at the appropriate time
and ask to speak to her. Determined, I sat waiting, seconds and

minutes, time shaping the four corners of the room. An hour passed: I needed to pick up the phone and place the call but could not.

Craning forward from my place on the couch, I stared into the bubbled glass of the television, burrowed inside myself, listening, watching, and waiting, trying to bring the facts into focus. The location. The collision had happened a short distance away from Michael Reese Hospital. The number of dead. The moment (1:33 p.m.) when the last three victims were pulled from the wreckage. I could envision, in my imagination, firefighters and EMTs combing for survivors through twisted smoking metal.

Because I had the mind of a writer even then, my imagination drew up grisly images that fleshed out the sanitized news reports. I sat through each added-to moment, my thoughts speeding up until I managed to calm down, only for them to speed up and cycle through my fear again.

On her days off from work—Sundays and holidays—my mother and I would catch the I.C. to the Loop, a smooth floating adventure, quiet and comfortable, preferable to the bus or El, and quicker, even if more expensive. I would watch the South Side unfurl outside the rattling window, houses and buildings soaring up and expanding in geometrical infinity, my spirits high—how exhilarating—then see Lake Michigan expand in vast offering, a flash of reflections, and more, until we slanted into the last station downtown. Buoyant, we might spend the day browsing the galleries at the Art Institute of Chicago—no matter how poor we were, my mother knew it was important to expose me to the larger world—then spend some time in Carson Pirie Scott or Marshall Field's, each department store housed in a spacious, beautiful building with marble walls and floors, stained glass, and other choice features, the best architecture that Chicago had to offer. Then we would go over to Wabash Avenue under the shadows of the El and eat dinner at Wendy's, my mother's favorite fast-food joint. The outing might end at Fannie May's with a small purchase of high-end caramel chews, turtles, and pecan rolls to enjoy on the I.C. home.

We were aligned. A nation of two. Her allegiances were to me. People often remarked how we looked alike, how we argued like husband and wife.

That evening, I heard my mother's heavy step climbing the carpeted wooden stairs, heard her pause on the landing before our front door, then a key turning the lock. Readying myself, praying. The door opened and there she was, my mother, another day, another dollar. Wobbly, I stood up from the couch. Dog-tired, she seemed to take some time to become aware of me. She glanced at me and promptly shut and locked the door behind her, not overly concerned about the TV blaring the news. I think I came toward her in a daze and held her, glad to find her body charged with life. She was a fleshy woman, just short of being fat, her arms thick, her hips branching wide. I was almost as tall as she was. (In a year or two, I would outgrow her, and she would often joke with her friends that she had to stand on a chair to "whup" me—my face buried in her bosom.)

She pulled me in, but she did not hold me for long. She was supportive, loving, but not affectionate.

She guided me back to the couch, and we sat for some minutes in silence, me breathing deeply, trying to console myself.

"Are you wheezing?" she asked.

I was not, but perhaps her words produced a dramatic effect in me and my lungs became more labored. Wheezing. This was her world, a poor single mother with a sickly child, no small burden at a time when the medical community did not know how to effectively treat the disease. Hours and days at my bedside—convalescence in the form of nights of a humidifier humming out cool air, Vicks VapoRub slathered across my chest—or at my gurney in an emergency room.

Already an anxious and melancholic child, the train crash loosed something in me, vague broodings. In the weeks that followed, I would lie in bed at night feeling like I was made of black air. At any time death could claim me. Worse, it could claim my mother. She did what she could to help comfort my fears. Then another disaster that December, an airline crash in the Everglades. I fixated on the reports, my mind looping through images of alligators springing up from black waters to feed on the survivors. But that was not the worst. A few days later, on the morning of January 1, 1973, I awakened to the news that Roberto Clemente, one of my favorite baseball players, had perished in a plane crash off the shores of Puerto Rico during an aid mission. It was the same tale being repeated.

See me and my mother standing at a bus stop on a cold winter night, my mother holding me close to her body, my face buried inside her wool coat. A scene frozen in time by a brutal Chicago winter, even if the weather was warmer than usual, the temperature above average. My mother protecting me from the elements and doing her best to protect me from an uncertain world.

Gospel hymns carried my mother through each day, songs of hope she sang to herself at home, songs that sustained her belief that God would safeguard and deliver us to the promised land of better times. But her faith felt foreign to me. We had been shortchanged. My mother struggled mightily to provide for us, the world cruel, unjust. By age seven I'd started to wonder why God would allow good people like her to suffer. And why did he allow foreign substances inside me to constrict my breathing (asthma), allow that constant surging, in the cell of my being, that filled me with feelings of black negativity? Fragile body, fragile mind.

Photographs reveal that by age nine I had stopped smiling, my mouth set to prevent others from viewing my buckteeth. This sense that I forever lived in the spotlight, the bright circle of public scrutiny, all eyes on me, even as (the flip side) I was given over to a sense that life was an elaborate stage set of actors and props, everything around me a clever performance.

That childish spell was broken when Bruce Lee died in July 1973, two weeks after my eleventh birthday, a tragedy that

had unexpected consequences for me. I'd heard much about the
martial arts icon but had never seen his films. That opportunity
came several months later. One morning, I caught the I.C. to the
Loop as I did each Saturday, but instead of attending my youth
class at the Art Institute, I paid two dollars to attend a Bruce Lee
marathon playing at a once-opulent movie house. I entered the
crowded theater, walked across a floor sticky beneath my shoes,
and for the better part of a day sat in a musty, tattered velvet seat,
gazing at the mammoth screen, watching and rewatching *Fist of
Fury*, *The Chinese Connection*, and *Enter the Dragon*, every punch,
kick, and growl implanted in my consciousness. Changed.

Even at that age I operated under the discipline of reading everything I could about any person or subject of interest,
a scholar's brain. Bruce Lee was no exception. Through Lee
my worldview expanded, took on new dimensions. So com-
pellingly did I envision a possibility for my life in his that I
decided to model myself after him. Eat what he ate. Train
the way he trained (impossible given that I frequently suffered
exercise-induced asthma attacks). Study and master every art
of combat the way he had. And like Lee, I would shake up the
world, then die in my prime.

The upshot of all this research was that I ventured into phi-
losophy for the first time, a scholastic add-on that provided a
frame for my feelings of discontentment and estrangement and
gave me much-needed confidence, bolstering me, bestowing a
sense of importance, a mission. Lee thought highly of Spinoza
and Krishnamurti, finding mindful equivalents to Jeet Kune
Do in their ideas. I read both men, although I couldn't make

heads or tails of Spinoza. Krishnamurti wrote for the layman, plain and direct. Immersing myself in his ideas, I embraced his view that "time"—the past, "thought"—was the cause of human suffering. I understood the truth that all traditions and orthodoxies—religious, philosophical, national, racial— amounted to little more than falsehoods that we must discard for an understanding of life in the moment. Sustained by the possibility that I could "free my mind from thought," a new conviction began to form.

Because something in me gravitated toward extremes, I became cavalier about my atheism, unconstrained and con- frontational, so much so that I sought every opportunity to antagonize a true believer: "If there is a God, let him strike me dead right now," words that often prompted the person to back away from me, to a safe distance. I was no longer in step with the world, but I convinced myself that I liked it that way.

I'm certain that my newfound disposition changed the way I was with my mother, certain that she worried about me but was at a loss as to what to say or do. A testing time. She was as gregarious as I was shy. She kept a circle of friends that in- cluded a dozen or more middle-aged Black women, mostly dayworkers like her. They abounded in a life of picnics, bar- becues, Tupperware parties, and club dates. I would observe, study, and judge them from the sidelines, their outbursts of laughter, impassioned eating and drinking, and cheerful gossip (what they called "Who-shot-John?"), me, an outsider, look- ing in at these interlopers.

At some point, she decided that enough was enough and

put her foot down, told me that I would be baptized, but when the Sunday came around, I refused to go to church and she did not force the issue. Perhaps I'd been counting on this outcome; she often gave in. Like other mothers of the time, she did not spare the rod, but she also tolerated much from me, allowed me free rein to backtalk and challenge her.

Perhaps I felt I could stand up to her because I believed she, a survivor of the Jim Crow South, did not stand up for herself, only took the indignities, insults, and injustices she suffered. Hard times had induced a stoic attitude toward life. For her, bygones were bygones. No looking back. No yesteryear nostalgia or disappointment.

I felt a need to protect her. More than once, my misguided chivalry would bring me into conflict with her employers.

Alone at home one Saturday I answered the phone. The man at the other end told me his name, a name that I recognized, that many would recognize. For decades his family had amassed wealth from operating a trucking company out of Chicago's stockyards. He asked to speak to my mother. I told him that she was away, not available.

"Tell your mother she better bring her black ass here right now," he said.

"Fuck you," I said.

"What did you say to me?"

If only I could have answered, cut him with my tongue. Instead, I said nothing.

"What did you say to me? On Monday I'll go down to the welfare office and have them cut off your aid."

Much shot through my mind. To have looked him in the face, seen his body. I wanted him to know me.

When my mother returned home, I told her about the exchange, told her I'd cussed out this dude, stupid racist jerk. She gave me her look, admonished me. From time to time, I'd heard my mother voice some displeasure about her employers, the rare complaint, but nothing she revealed was lost on me, a catalog of wrongs stored within, fueling my anger, justifying the longed-for comeuppance, payback.

Later that day, the man called again, this time to apologize. As it turned out, the wife had given my mother the day off but had miscommunicated the fact to him, an honest mistake. My mother knew this meant his wife had spent the day in an alcoholic stupor, facts forgotten. She accepted his apology, but his insult was the straw that broke the camel's back, her polite tone at odds with the way she felt. She found some excuse to never return to their home.

It would be many years before I understood that around my mother's sober acceptance of the status quo was a whole culture she had developed for our subsistence and well-being that I knew nothing about. As a survivor of the segregated South, she had already seen it all. More than one man in our family had been lynched in Mississippi. Seeking greener pastures, she'd made the Great Migration to Chicago in 1949 when she

was nineteen years old, greeted on arrival by the odor of the
stockyards and slick city life. A witness, she was one among
thousands of Black folk who viewed Emmett Till's body on
public display inside a glass-fronted coffin. ("It was horrible,"
she said.) Although white people would forever be a threat, her
immediate concerns were the mortal dangers of South Side
Chicago that she had to contend with each day, an exigency
that overrode any reluctance she felt about carrying a Saturday
night special.

She started carrying the pistol after she and her boyfriend
John were robbed at gunpoint one night outside our courtyard
building in the fall of 1974. Making light of a terrifying moment, she would recount the story of how John refused to take
off his college graduation ring and how the two thugs grew
impatient.

The vocal one spoke: "Lady, you better tell this nigger to
take off his ring before I shoot him."

Hearing her tell it, my mother's friends—practical
women—would shake their heads and laugh in disbelief. But I
silently applauded John's stubborn resistance.

To a bookish child like me, John made an overpowering
impression of learning and intelligence. His style and manner, his dignity and unassuming demeanor, were far removed
from the "cool" that many Black men thought necessary to
display in public. I can still see him sitting on our living room
couch in suit and tie, smoking a pipe with a soft expression of
curiosity on his smooth, dark-skinned face—I would chance
upon his pipe cleaners and golf ball holders secreted around

our apartment—his sideburns seeming to anchor a short Afro to his head. He was soft-spoken and thoughtful like no other person I'd met.

He and my mother often argued, but I never heard him raise his voice, only concede after so many insults. "Well, Alice, I don't know why you had to say that."

I suspect that my mother met him at the welfare office where he pulled a nine-to-five as a "case" (social) worker. Men were one side of my mother's practical character. In addition to John, she kept two other main squeezes in rotation, L.C. and Eddie, although other male companions came and went—like the one who gave her a run-of-the-mill Expressionist painting that she hung for some years before gifting it to a friend—men all unalike from one another, their lives overlapping via my mother. John, Eddie, and L.C. shared one tragic trait: each man succumbed to a terminal disease before his time.

Tuberculosis claimed L.C. (After he died, my mother and I were required to follow a regimen of preventive medication for a year.) As I remember him, L.C. was an older man, well into his sixties; he looked like a well-used Kewpie doll, his hair flaring above his head in a wavy perm (speeding jellyfish), his face round but severe, mapped with age and wrinkles. He presented an imposing figure but without any display of muscle, his waist so wide that his legs seemed too slim to sustain his bulk. If John was urbane, L.C. was country in his unapologetic speech and dress, like a hunter who had simply materialized on city streets. Joining in my memory with the smell of oil and bleach, the wood-paneled station wagon he drove was filled with tools—he provided us with a steady supply of Drano, light-bulbs, screws and nails, hammers and hacksaws, and electrical tape and sandpaper—and in its extended length and design resembled a cross between a trailer home and a funeral hearse.

To the best of my knowledge, L.C. never learned about my mother's involvement with other men, although in my plain-spoken innocence I sometimes betrayed her confidences.

I did so one time when Eddie was rooted next to me on the couch, his black-socked feet crossed on the floor, and the edge of his reading glasses case poking up from the pocket of his dress shirt. He was short and slight, his small shoulders bearing his oval-shaped head, his hair cut close to the scalp, his mustache pencil-thin like an Easter egg adornment. Mostly a quiet man, that day he kept up a steady stream of chatter throughout an episode of *Star Trek* airing on the boxy console color television he'd bought for me and my mother. Every few minutes he would grin and butt in: "I don't like that phony stuff." (He often found my interests and activities perplexing. For example, he would see me hovering over a chessboard moving both the white and black pieces and would look at me as if he'd caught me masturbating.)

Near the end of the episode, I asked him if he knew John. He directed his gaze at the floor. "John?"

"Yeah," I said. "He was here the other night watching *Hawaii Five-O.*"

Later, my mother shared my gaffe with her friends. It became a standing joke in our family, like the fact that Eddie always bought us a stunted Christmas tree no taller than him.

He was with us on the regular—at our apartment, taking us on errands in his LTD, even attending social events—so much so that I spent more time in his company than with any other man during my adolescence. Always on standby for my mother. When she needed him, she would instruct my cousin Charles—seven years older than me—to call his home and pretend to be a running buddy from the Indiana steel mill where he worked. Back then, it never occurred to me that he and my mother were having an "affair." I had no sense of the rightness or wrongness of any of it. Once inside our apartment, he would remove his shoes at the door then stand akimbo in his black socks (small feet peeking out like two mice from beneath his slacks), ready to be of service to "Alice May," his term of endearment for my mother; before he put on his shoes to leave, he would often slip my mother some cash, a few crisp bills.

What financial lines were drawn between these three men? What limits set?

One afternoon during my junior year in high school, John came to collect me and my mother in his clean, comfortable car. I marveled at the news that we were going to purchase a new stereo system, my elevated spirits carrying me through the car ride to the electronics store. In memory I move through sliding glass doors, a salesman quick to latch on to me in high excitement. We converse, the salesman appraising our needs—I'd done my research—then I'm borne across glazed floor tiles on his undulating voice, John and my mother trailing behind us, the store flooded with LED illumination flowing

out from stereo equipment perched in tiers along the wall, a
watery resonance, the air glittering with music—disco, funk,
R&B, rock. After an hour, I'd selected a receiver, turntable,
cartridge and needle, tape deck, and speakers, edging over the
thousand-dollar budget John had set. But I was not satisfied.

Credit card in hand, John accompanied the salesman to the
cash register. I seized the moment, told my mother, "We need
an equalizer."

She said nothing, only started for the register. I repeated
my demand. She continued walking as if she hadn't heard me,
but once we reached the register there was a nod and a lift of
the head, the flashing of her look, and that was the end of it.

On the ride home, I stewed in the back seat, dissatisfied,
ungrateful, sullen, evil-eyeing my mother, evil-eyeing John.
Nothing but ease in John's handling of the car, elbow crooked
on the edge of the open window, tips of his finger controlling
the steering wheel. Then something moved in his gaze, barely
noticeable. Other movement followed. Every now and then,
his head and arms crackling with tremors like the starting
of a small avalanche in his body, symptoms of the multiple
sclerosis that would cut him down a few years later, still in
his forties.

Lung cancer cut Eddie down a few years after the steel mill
cheated him out of his pension. Fired him before his twenty-
fifth year on the job, bequeathing him nothing more than two
decades of exposure to toxic materials.

I no long remember how my mother took the loss, or
John's or L.C.'s, only that there were no more boyfriends after

Eddie. What has stayed with me is the full display of grief after
her mother's death.

In the fall of 1979, at the start of my senior year in high school,
my grandmother took the train up from the South to visit. I
knew that she was sick, battling stomach cancer. She'd already
endured a hard sixty-six years. Raised on a sharecropping
plantation, then by her late teens embarking with her sisters on
daywork, the profession they passed on to my mother and aunt.
As I knew her, she was a glum, serious woman who offered
little in the way of kindness to me and my cousins when we
spent our summers with her in West Memphis, quick to criticize and punish, showing cruelty even in the large tablespoon
of cod-liver oil she made each one of us take every morning.

Her visit was mostly uneventful. She slept on the sleeper
sofa in our living room. We would sit together watching her
favorite TV programs, *Sanford and Son* and *The Waltons*. I was
full of feelings but mostly aware of her overworked wig that
never quite fit, gray hairs weeding out, her slack, tired face,
her mouth puckered without her false teeth, her sandbag-like
flabby arms, and her calves covered in liver spots. We rarely
spoke during the weeks she visited, so I was surprised one day
when she opened up and advised me, "Don't be a wallflower."
On the morning of her return home, she paused packing her
suitcase, pointed at my chess trophies on display, and started
sobbing, proud, my accomplishments harbingers of a better
tomorrow for our family.

A few months later, I dreamed about her one night. This last time I saw her, she was thin, emaciated, seated next to me on my bed. She spoke to me: "I won't be seeing you anymore." I hugged her, felt the bones beneath her skin, and cried.

The next morning, my mother told me that she'd died the previous night. Then my mother said, "Now I have no one."

I did not understand what she meant. Was I not someone? Were we not a nation of two?

Only now, forty years later, do I begin to feel what she felt, circling to an understanding, the great fear of my childhood realized.

I enter the nursing home, make my way to the "day room," where I find my mother parked at a table in her wheelchair, her ninety years deposited in this leather-and-steel contraption under the direction of two rubber wheels circumscribing her days.

She mostly asks me questions. "My mother's name was Addie? . . . I had one brother? . . . He was killed? . . . I have one sister? . . . She had four kids but one of them died? . . . One of my nephews is named Larry? . . . He does them drugs? . . . Did you ever do them drugs?"

Then, looking befuddled, she asks me, "Jeffery, what do we do now?"

"Nothing," I say. "We just sit here."

"We just sit here?"

"Yes."

She accepts my answer, then directs her gaze back to the television mounted on the wall, only to repeat the question a few minutes later.

Nothing I can do to save her. No way to pull her from the wreckage of time and disease. Nothing I can do to save myself from the sunken place of grief. "Now I have nobody."

At the Horizon

MAGGIE SHIPSTEAD

When I was twenty-five, I lived on Nantucket for eight months, through a winter. I'd decided to go because I was writing a novel set on a thinly disguised version of the island, and I had some fellowship money from the graduate program I'd just finished, almost enough for the relatively cheap off-season. I didn't have anywhere else to be. I thought I would meet people.

I didn't. To be fair, there weren't a ton to meet. The only other inhabited house on my street was shabby and spooky, its yard thickly layered with fallen leaves. An electric glow seeped from the back, but the front rooms were always dark. Sometimes I saw flashlight beams moving around inside. When I looked up the address in the local crime blotter, I learned that the owner had been arrested two years previously for stealing two hundred dollars from a disabled person. Once, I parked alongside the fence and later found a KitKat bar and a tennis ball stuck among the pickets—offerings for me and my dog, Boo Radley–style.

Even when I might have connected with a fellow human,

I quickly got so out of practice making chitchat that I started to shy away. There was a stretch of five weeks when I didn't have a single face-to-face conversation beyond buying a coffee or groceries. I became rigidly attached to my daily routine, irrationally anxious about accomplishing simple tasks, terrified of being conspicuous. I was a shy child, and shy people often think other people are paying closer attention to them than they are. Taking my trash to the island dump, I fretted I would somehow mess up, that people would see my ineptitude and judge me, know I didn't belong. But the dump was not complicated, and no one noticed or cared what I did.

The natural beauty I saw while walking my dog—the frozen ponds and snowy beaches, the tender pale sunsets over whitecapped ocean—sometimes felt irrelevant, even discouraging, without anyone else to stand there with me and say something like, *Wow, so pretty.* I'd first come to the island with an ex-boyfriend, and I thought about him a lot. At the end of my conversation-free five weeks, two friends came to visit. I motormouthed at them until they pleaded exhaustion. In the middle of the night, when my friend Bobby passed through my bedroom to get to the bathroom, I startled awake and sat bolt upright in bed, screaming.

But, slowly, without realizing it, I was being changed. The gray and windy winter on a street of shuttered houses seemed to inoculate me against loneliness. I don't think I'm actually immune—I don't think anyone is—but at least I wasn't afraid of being lonely anymore, and that was almost the same thing. After Nantucket, I started to seek out solitude, to relish it.

A convert's zealousness shows in a piece I wrote for a magazine about solo travel: *I've stood alone on a hilltop under a total solar eclipse. I've stood beside a frozen lake under the speeding green plumes of the aurora borealis. I've floated in the South Pacific above a humpback whale while its song reverberated in my ribs. There are people I love who I wish had experienced these things, too, but if I'd waited for them, I wouldn't have done any of it.*

We're told memories are best when they're shared, but I'm saying sometimes it's okay to gobble down the world like the most delicious midnight snack, all for you. I'm saying our memories are only ever really our own, anyway. I'm saying: take a trip.

The trip I most want to take is a 270-mile solo hike in the Swedish Arctic, a trail called the Kungsleden. There are communal huts you can stay in on parts of the trail, but I will sleep in my tent, which is ultralight and sized for one person. I planned to go last year but got derailed by a magazine gig. This year the coronavirus pandemic will almost definitely rule it out. From within the enforced aloneness of quarantine, I'm dreaming of freely chosen solitude.

In 1934, the polar explorer Richard E. Byrd decided to spend an Antarctic winter alone in a hut a hundred miles from where the other members of his expedition were hunkered down in the relative snugness of their base on the edge of the Ross Ice Shelf. Initially, he claimed his purpose was to make meteorological observations through the breathtakingly harsh and dark winter, but in the opening of his book about the experience,

Alone, he admits he also wanted "to taste peace and quiet and solitude long enough to find out how good they really are." He imagined a season of peaceful contemplation and study accompanied only by the wind, the aurora, and the sound of his phonograph. He would place his body in a remote, hostile location, and then retreat even further into his own inner recesses to see what he found. Byrd's intentions might have been earnest, but he was also publicity savvy. He knew government sponsorship of his expeditions depended on his continued fame, and he knew a solitary Antarctic winter would make for heroic press.

In the end, Byrd spent four and a half months in a snow-buried hut that he called Advance Base, but he found little peace. Snow and ice continually clogged his ventilator pipes and accumulated on top of his trapdoor to the surface, threatening to entomb him. Vastly compounding the problem, his heater was leaking carbon monoxide. He fell into a deep depression and was tormented by lethargy, night terrors, and physical pain. Eventually, alarmed by his increasingly incoherent Morse transmissions, members of his expedition set out to rescue him. Under the best of circumstances, crossing the crevassed Ross Ice Shelf is no picnic, and making the journey during late-winter twilight, in extreme cold and with severe storms a constant threat, was incredibly dangerous. They succeeded. Byrd was retrieved and survived, though he never fully recovered from the effects of carbon monoxide poisoning, either in body or mind.

I wonder sometimes if the price of my heightened resistance to loneliness might be higher than I realize. I'm in the phase of life when there are a lot of weddings, a lot of first babies, when, to many, the absence of those things appears troublesome, even pitiable. People like to say you have to be happy alone before you can be happy with someone else, but that doesn't seem true. I know plenty of people who *hated* being alone and whose happiness in finding a partner was magnified by relief. Their dislike, sometimes even horror, of being alone primed them for love, motivated them to commit. But if you're actually happy alone, if you've accomplished that mythical prerequisite for love, you will probably also have rendered love less necessary, made yourself less amenable to accommodating someone's needs and schedule and foibles. You run the risk of becoming set in your ways, of being unable *not* to feel smothered.

An acupuncturist, feeling my pulse, said he could tell I was an armored person. I asked my mom later if she thought I was armored, and she laughed like, *duh*. Would I be able to tell the difference between contentment and armor? It seems like one should be light and the other heavy, but you can get used to weight, not even notice it after a while.

Loneliness has more varied causes than lack of romantic love, but that is the conspicuously and chronically empty social category in my life. Usually I don't mind. Usually I would say I prefer my freedom. But there have been times (for instance, at a wedding where I didn't know many people and slunk away when the dancing started) when gloom has suffused my inner atmosphere, when a voice has whispered that if only I had someone, *anyone*, then I wouldn't feel like this. But that's just a trick of the brain. A lie. All the relationships I've had in the past decade have been long-distance, and I've still managed to feel smothered. I will meet a man somewhere after a long separation, make a joyful reunion, and then quickly find myself wishing I were alone so I could enjoy myself.

I have a what-if, though, a what-might-have-been. Years ago, I became immediately and precipitously infatuated with a man I'd just met, absorbed by him in a way I hadn't experienced before and haven't again. We spent one night together. He already had a partner, an established life, and the next day he returned to them. When I've gone back to the city where we met, I've found the whole place saturated with loneliness. It seeps into my body but also weakens with time, as though following a schedule of decay, a half-life.

In the Chernobyl Exclusion Zone, the thousand square miles around the melted-down reactor where human activity is forbidden, wild animals thrive in the radioactive landscape, given sanctuary by disaster. Remote cameras transmit their images: boars, wolves, roe deer, eagles and storks, even European brown bears, not seen in the region for almost a hundred years. The term *involuntary park*, coined by science fiction writer Bruce Sterling, refers to a place that we humans have inadvertently returned to nature by rendering it unfit for ourselves. The demilitarized zone between North and South Korea is another one. It's 2.5 miles wide and 155 miles long, edged with fences, walls, sentry towers, land mines. But rare birds and the Asiatic black bear live inside; some even think stealthy Siberian tigers and Amur leopards pad through that narrow strip of perfect wilderness.

The lost possibility of that man did not leave a void. The space he would have occupied is filled with other things. The experiences I listed in that piece about solo travel—the aurora and the whales, the eclipse—were made possible by the life I have instead. Zones of unexpected wilderness, places that have been left *alone*, excite me. New possibilities thrive, grow thick.

Someday, I might have a different kind of life. Our potential paths through time and space are complex and resolutely unpredictable. No one can tell us the possible consequences of even our smallest choices; no one can live our lives for us. We have a basic and innate responsibility for ourselves that can't be sloughed off, no matter how hard we try, and that seems like an immovable solitude to me. We are contained within our bodies and minds, and although we can use both to connect with other people, to feel close, that closeness is finite. Maybe the impossibility of perfect togetherness, of perfect understanding, is what makes the search for connection so enticing, the moments of resonance so profound.

Solitude stands sentry at the horizons of our lives. We enter and leave the world alone, and what are we to make of the fact that the only two truly universal experiences are also the only ones nobody will ever be able to tell us about?

I've never had a particularly close brush with death, at least not that I'm aware of. But there was that small plane forced lower and lower over the Arctic Ocean by bad weather, the pilot's grim concentration as he tried and failed three times to land in a strong crosswind. There was that car I got into in Delhi with strange men after I got separated from my friend, how I thought they would drive me around the corner and instead they drove me out of the city. These things turned out fine, but they might not have. Probably there are many other moments that went unnoticed, when I was at the mercy of chance and other people.

There have been times, too, when it's been up to me. I've found myself at crossroads where, in retrospect, I can see that a path not taken seems to make a beeline for that mysterious final horizon. On a travel magazine assignment in the Maldives, for example, an hour after I finished an ordinary scuba dive to sixty feet, an electric rip ran down the center of my vision. Numbness started traveling up the right side of my body. This was horrible but not unfamiliar: I know the progression of my migraine symptoms. After the numbness comes garbled speech, muddied thoughts, then an awl boring through the left side of my head. At first I didn't realize something different was happening. A dull pain like muscle fatigue spread through the fatty parts of my body: my butt and hips, my breasts. Maybe the dive had tired me out more than I thought? But then my joints started to ache. An itchy, stinging rash speckled my torso. For hours, all I could do was endure, try to nap. The ship's doctor was elderly and French and spoke little English. He assured me I had sunstroke. When I said I hadn't been in the sun, he smiled patiently and suggested I take an ibuprofen, drink water. Through my pain and addled cognition, I didn't know how to do anything beyond acquiesce.

Later, I realized I'd been experiencing a mild but still excruciating case of decompression sickness, or the bends. The bends happen when the nitrogen that accumulates in your blood during a dive doesn't have time to be safely exhaled (usually because of a rushed ascent) and instead bubbles out through your tissues. The consequences can be severe, even fatal. Divers like to think the bends are 100 percent avoidable if certain rules are followed, that only the incompetent are at risk, but that's not true. Your odds of decompression sickness can be drastically reduced through careful dive practices, but unpredictable physiological factors are in play. For instance, 20 to 25 percent of people have a perforation between the two atria of their heart that, for most, causes no ill effects, even when diving, but for some—and I suspect probably me—correlates both with aura migraines and increased chances of decompression sickness even after moderate, benign dives.

Sometimes mild symptoms become abruptly, dangerously worse if untreated. Breathing oxygen may help; a trip to a recompression chamber might be necessary. My symptoms happened to get better on their own, though my body felt bruised and sore for days. That night I sought out the divemaster and explained what had happened. I told him I needed to cancel my dive for the next day.

He insisted I was wrong. "The dive was perfectly safe," he

said. "Your problem is something else. But if you don't want to dive, that's up to you."

He was right in that we'd been well within the standard safety parameters. I suspected he didn't want to entertain the possibility of a decompression problem because he thought I would blame him. I didn't. In elite cave diver Jill Heinerth's memoir *Into the Planet*, she describes a severe episode of the bends that, when I read it months later, made my skin prickle first with recognition and then anger that no one on the ship had believed me. Her decompression sickness was far worse than mine, as her dive had been at the extremes of both duration and depth (though not out of the ordinary for her), but her account of the sensation was eerily, unmistakably familiar: the itchy rash, the bone-deep soreness, the exhaustion, the sense of wrongness. "I felt a crippling terror," she wrote, "afraid that if I moved, I might set a bubble loose in my circulation that would paralyze or kill me. That's what makes the bends so insidious. A diver might only ever experience a minor rash, but someone else could be unlucky enough to have a single bubble get trapped in a very bad place like the spinal cord or brain."

I hesitated, staring at the divemaster. I hate feeling like I'm being cowardly or weak, like I'm a child again, cooking up some farfetched excuse to get out of PE. To dive again the day after an incident of the bends would have been exceptionally dangerous. Still, I found myself genuinely considering going down again. But why? Just to prove to this man, this stranger, that I wasn't a wimp, whatever that meant? If anything, I was more likely to end up proving to him, catastrophically, that I'd been right. Still, there would have been something comforting in agreeing that, yes, I'd just had sunstroke, yielding to his dive expertise, following along. I felt suddenly, hopelessly lonely. I couldn't take what had happened in my body and make it concrete and visible. I couldn't hold it in front of his face as proof. The pain was mine alone, as was the decision about what to do next. I knew he and the doctor thought I was being hysterical, and the fact that they were wrong didn't stop me from feeling embarrassed, even ashamed.

"I don't think I should," I said.

"It's your choice," he said, shrugging.

When people are in survival situations or the midst of trauma, a certain phenomenon occurs with surprising frequency. An external human presence appears, offering some combination of companionship, encouragement, and guidance. (John Geiger wrote a book about it called *The Third Man Factor*.) The presence may speak and be active or may simply hover at the edge of someone's consciousness, keeping company, staving off despair. It may be a known, recognizable person—often a relative or a friend, almost always dead—or it may be faceless and genderless. One of the most famous instances was the feeling shared by Ernest Shackleton and his two companions that someone else had been with them as they crossed the glaciers and mountains of South Georgia Island at the desperate end of their quest for rescue after their ship *Endurance* was crushed by ice. Joshua Slocum, the first man to sail around the world alone, described in his account of the voyage an incident in which, while he was incapacitated by food poisoning, a ghostly crew member from Christopher Columbus's ship the *Pinta* steered his little sloop until he recovered. The last person to exit the South Tower of the World Trade Center before it collapsed on September 11, 2001, felt a presence guiding him down the stairwell, urging him to climb over rubble and walk through fire. Similar stories abound among mountaineers, soldiers, astronauts, shipwreck survivors—people who, intentionally or not, have found themselves at a place of extremity.

Some explain these visitations as guardian angels sent by God. Others hypothesize that the brain might be vividly manifesting a companion to help itself through debilitating stress, generating an angel from within. It strikes me as beautiful and heartbreaking that these people didn't hallucinate a meal or a warm bed or some other useful object or source of material comfort that would, in its unreality, also be akin to surrender. (If you lie down in an imaginary bed while trying to descend a mountain in a snowstorm, you will not be getting back up.) No, what they wanted most was simply not to be alone, and once they didn't *feel* alone, even though they were, the survivors found the inner grit to keep going. In many accounts, the presence disappears as soon as survival is ensured, its work done.

The connection and closeness we can achieve with another person is finite, but these manifested companions embody the power of human connection, how we crave it and draw strength from our bond with others. The brain, in these examples, is essentially casting a spell of protection in the form of another human, seeking relief from the lonely burden of self-reliance. What a relief to yield to a firm, reassuring authority, to have someone to trust, to save energy by finding calm, even if the authority is not actually separate from the self. No one knows, of course, if people who don't survive might also feel a presence. If they do, I hope it stays until the end, so they don't feel alone when they die, even if they are. If I ever find myself alone on a mountain or lost at sea, nearing the vanishing point on the horizon, I hope someone will come to keep me company, even if it's only myself.

Exodus, 2020

EMILY RABOTEAU

First to abandon our building in upper Manhattan was A., the fact-checker from apartment 5. She defected with her twin daughters in late March, at the start of the curve. I saw her the night before they fled, down in the basement laundry room, frantically shoving heaps of dirty clothes into all four washers. Her panic was stoked by the city's rapid spread of contagion and the demagogue's threat to close state borders. Now she was perseverating on the worst-case scenario, not bothering to separate whites from darks. Who could blame her? A thousand New Yorkers had already died. Since the schools had shut down, her life as a single working parent had become unsustainable. She performed her job badly at night, online, after the girls fell asleep. Absent childcare or a partner with whom to share the burden, A. was running on empty, wearing mismatched shoes.

The plan was to drive to Connecticut where her elderly parents lived, A. said. She'd blow her emergency savings self-quarantining in an Airbnb for two weeks before moving in with them. If this wasn't an emergency, she didn't know what was. She'd requested a rental car with Connecticut plates, in case highway patrolmen tried to turn her back at the state line. A. and her twins would walk all the way to the Bronx to pick up the car, the farthest they'd ever walked, since the subway system had become a vector of the disease. But, my neighbor confessed, she had no plan for the girls' guardianship if she were already infected. What if she were to die of the virus? If the children were infected, too, her parents could not risk taking them on. Her sister lived all the way in California and might not be able to fly under the shifting guidelines. In that grim eventuality, A. feared, setting the washers on "heavy load," her girls would become temporary wards of the state.

I promised we would watch after them, until her sister arrived. Of course we would. What else was community for but this? Her children were friends with our children; she could trust us to keep them safe. "Thank you for saying that," she cried. Then she gave me her spare keys with permission to raid her refrigerator, apologized for the mess in 5, and was gone. Weeks later, I found a little pink sock, furred with lint, underneath one of the dryers and presumed she'd dropped it in her haste. By that point the twenty-four-hour subway system had shut down for sanitization from the early morning hours of 1:00 to 5:00 a.m., the milk in A.'s fridge had rotted, packages were being stolen from the lobby, and half the building had fled.

Next to go were B. and Z., a middle school teacher and a forensic lawyer from apartment 34. Z. texted me to ask a favor before they migrated with their young children to Rhode Island to live with her sister. This was at the start of April. I hoped they needed us to watch their cat. We'd catsat before, when their family went on vacations. Having an animal to nurture would help us through these disruptions to normalcy, I thought. No, Z. replied, they were taking the cat. She couldn't say when they'd be back. She'd arranged to have their mail forwarded to her sister's address but wondered if I could shove any packages already en route inside 34. She was expecting a few boxes, one which I was welcome to take, from a food service called Thrive.

Of course, I told Z., though it felt like a small insult that her family was leaving. I didn't exactly resent them for making this choice. Three thousand and five hundred New Yorkers had died. But their departure gave me misgivings for hazarding to stay. *We're tougher than them*, I steeled myself. *We're real New Yorkers, sucking it up and staying put.* In truth, I was scared of giving or getting COVID-19, mourning our neighborhood's shuttered stores as well as the deaths of colleagues and neighbors, but we had nowhere else to go. Part of me envied Z.'s escape plan—the part that wanted my children to thrive. Another part of me wanted to witness the city's transformation and participate in its rebuilding—the part committed to the common good. Z. sent her husband up to the sixth floor to give us a set of their keys. I registered the stricken look on B.'s face. At that point in the pandemic, we weren't yet wearing masks as a rule; the full range of grief was on display, from disbelief to despair. B. looked bereft, like a man who'd just been caught betraying his wife.

"Stay strong, brother," my husband encouraged him. "We'll see you on the other side." He meant this as a kindness, presuming the pandemic's end and our neighbors' eventual return. But I was beginning to wonder, What if they never came back?

That month, in inverse proportion to the mounting death toll, the building continued emptying out. Those who had the means to leave left. Who knew so many people had second homes or family with ample enough space to take them in? Unlike A., B., and Z., most of our neighbors never said goodbye. P. and K., the composer and his wife who served on the building's board, defected for their summer home, also in Connecticut. I missed running into them in the elevator with their arthritic dog, V. They'd neglected to turn off their alarm clock. We heard it beeping without end through the adjoining wall to apartment 61, a reminder of their absence and the general state of alarm.

R. and L., classics professors nearing retirement, took refuge from apartment 66 at their cabin in the Catskills. How was it possible that I even missed R. making lewd remarks down by the mailboxes, with liquor on his breath? Before she put apartment 64 on the market after losing her editorial job, D. brought us some of the corn bread she'd baked as something to do to fill time. The movies always made the end of the world look action-packed, she remarked, whereas this apocalypse was boring.

I'm not sure where M. went, the piano teacher from apartment 45, nor T., a bassist with the New York Philharmonic who lived in 24. All I know is that I missed the flights of the music I used to hear through the air shaft when they practiced their instruments. In place of those scales grew the sirens of ambulances racing to the hospital, several times an hour. I stopped seeing the sweet old woman, E., from apartment 63, always dressed for church. J., our super, informed me that she was now on dialysis, having been carried out on a stretcher. Those of us who remained hung out the windows at seven o'clock, madly cheering on the essential workers and banging on empty pots. *Stay alive*, chanted one of my children, marching in circles around the messy living room. His older sibling packed a backpack of stuffed animals and announced he was running away to live with his friends because he was sick and tired of the quarantine—but all of his friends had gone. There was nowhere to run to but the closet, where I later discovered him making signs for a detective agency. *Mysteries Solved $1. Missing Persons Will Be Found.*

In mid-April, I contacted H., the young rabbi from apartment 41, to ask if his pregnant wife, Y., had borne the baby yet. Ten thousand New Yorkers had died. Scores of corpses were piled in mass graves in a potter's field off the Bronx or stacked in refrigerated trucks to ease the burden on funeral homes and morgues. At the same time, others were being born. I wanted to see the baby, to be near new life, even if it wasn't safe for me to smell her head.

H.'s cell number was handwritten on a piece of blue stationery he'd taped earlier that spring to the elevator mirror: *Hey Neighbors! If you're sick, elderly, or otherwise unable to leave your apartment, I'm happy to help drop off food/stuff in front of your door. Take care!* Such a kindness. Since the note was still there, I assumed he and Y. and their two toddlers were, too. If their baby was born, I knew from experience that H. and Y. would be the ones in need of such kindness now. I offered to prepare some kosher meals they could keep in their freezer and reheat in a pinch. No need, H. announced. The baby had indeed arrived—a girl they'd named R.; she and Y. were doing well, all things considered, and he hoped we were, too—but they had left New York.

How to describe the particular loneliness of this—of having been jilted along with the metropolis, by the loose acquaintances who make up the pattern of a life? On the island of Manhattan, where we live cheek to jowl, there are over seventy thousand of us per square mile. My building has six stories and forty-four units. Some of us are poor. Some of us aren't. I know everyone who lives here, by sight if not by name. In particular, I know the other families with children. My kids were both born in our apartment. My husband prepared the neighbors above, below, and to either side of us for the animal sounds of my labor by slipping notes under their doors, so they wouldn't hear me crying through the walls and think I was hurt. At times, I have thought the building is alive, but of course that is wrong. We who live here make it so.

When my firstborn arrived, a decade ago, J. came up from apartment 23 to deliver a baby gift, a little blue elephant. I recognized it a few years later sitting atop the dresser of R. in apartment 32 when I went over to show her how to breastfeed her own baby. I assumed she found it in the basement Trash to Treasure nook, where I'd traded it for some hand-me-down toy another neighbor's child had outgrown. Such was the flow of cooperative living and the language of mutual aid. *Can I borrow an egg? Can you feed my cat? Your toilet is causing a leak in my ceiling. Here, I made extra.*

Last Mother's Day, those of us with little kids planted a potted garden in the alleyway where the building's garbage and recycling bins are kept, so there'd be a green space to gather and play in. Was that only a year ago? We planted impatiens, hosta, and ferns, plants that would survive the shade of the building next door, so close that we only enjoyed a narrow strip of sky. We agreed to take turns keeping the garden alive. We bought benches and an outdoor table set with a bright umbrella. We strung solar lights along the concertina wire at the top of the chain link fence. Our kids played hopscotch down there, rode scooters, threw water balloons.

This Mother's Day, the death toll in New York was 21,517. By then, the only other kids left in the building were the pre-teenagers H. and K., whose mother, I., took up smoking again after losing her job as an importer of Turkish bedsheets. She stopped riding the elevator with us because it wasn't possible to socially distance in that box, but sometimes when I threw out the trash, I'd catch her in the untended garden, furtively stubbing out a cigarette in one of the dirt-filled pots. One time she asked me if I wanted to buy a kid's bike. It was too small for H. and K., but maybe for one of my boys? Under normal circumstances, she would have just given me the bike for free, she said, but now they needed the money. She quoted her price and I bought it on the spot.

After that the new ritual was to meet in the nearest park

with T., mother of one of my son's first-grade classmates, while our boys practiced bike riding in wobbly circles on the once-crowded, now-deserted blacktop. The first time we broke quarantine to arrange such a playdate, in late May, T. and I both felt giddy, as starved for social interaction as our sons, and as out of practice. This became our afternoon reprieve from a season without structure or haircuts, trapped in our buildings with our nuclear families, in a city with so many dying and dead. She often brought me coffee. We'd sit at opposite ends of a bench with our masks pulled down to talk. We agreed that though our children learned nothing remotely at home after their public school shut down, and despite them losing even more stimulation without the prospect of summer camp, we should at least feel accomplished in the time of corona for teaching them to ride bicycles.

T.'s family had suffered the virus early in its spread. Having recovered, she felt fairly certain that their antibodies gave them immunity from contracting COVID-19 again or from the risk of spreading it further on a flight from the city, though the science on this was still fuzzy. She was planning a summer vacation in San Diego for three weeks in July. It would be easier there, she imagined. More space. More liberty. Less restrictions. Less death. The zoo was open, and so was the beach. She couldn't stand it here anymore, she said. The rats. The increase in crime. The closure of everything cultural. "New York is dead." That's what she said. People were saying that, then. But we're still here, I insisted. Even with half a million people gone, we were still a city of 8 million. I didn't blame

T. for wanting to get out until she called from California in August to say they weren't coming back. By that point, my second-born's bike had been stolen.

I can't remember exactly when it was that N., my old roommate, called to check in. Twenty years ago, in our rail-road apartment on Seventh above a taqueria, she entertained at night a parade of boyfriends in a tiny bedroom she'd painted red, while temping and going on auditions in the day. Now she'd decamped to her parents' second home in New Jersey, doubting her abilities to keep her teenage children safe under lockdown in Brooklyn. They'd been gone from the city for a long time, long enough that it didn't seem to me like she was from here anymore.

"How is it there?" she asked me.

This might have been around the time the medical director of the local ER killed herself, unable to handle the magnitude of loss.

"It's lonely," I said. Quite simply, I missed the garden as it had been, when all of us were in it.

N. was incredulous. She told me I didn't know the mean-ing of loneliness. She described the cul-de-sac of the planned community where her nuclear family had been stuck in a house without character for months on end like that Sartre play we read in college—*No Exit*. There were no sidewalks, she said, nowhere to go, nobody in that purgatory went outside except to get into their car to go on their biweekly grocery run. It was a sensory-deprivation chamber without diversity, interconnec-tion, or frisson. She pined for the city like for an ex-lover. She said she would give her right arm just to see another human being, even a passing stranger; just for the chance to buy an avocado at a bodega, or eavesdrop, or walk down Broadway among other city dwellers, no matter how pushy, for five or ten blocks.

There are many ways to be lonely. Even in a crowd. There could be as many reasons why people left the city as there are ways to be lonely within it. They were scared of getting infected or of infecting others. They had not enough money or too much. They were pushed away or pulled. They dreamed of better prospects or woke up to a nightmare. Maybe N. and the others will come back. Maybe they won't. I can't say. But N. made me see I'd been taking certain privileges for granted. This much I can say: Yesterday, when my friend S. helped me carry home the farm-share vegetables from the pickup spot in Harlem forty blocks away, I introduced him to L. from apartment 1, who was heading out the door with her two little dogs, but not before asking if my son G. would like to help her walk them later that evening, knowing how much he loves animals, and reporting that J., the super, had dragged the potted plants from the alley into the basement to protect them from impending tropical storm I., since, being perennials, they had returned.

Maine Man

LEV GROSSMAN

The nearest I've ever come to losing my mind was in the fall of 1991 in a small town in Maine called Ellsworth.

I was twenty-two, just out of college. I'd spent the summer after graduation in Boston working on a travel guide to Mexico, but I knew that wasn't what I wanted to do with my life. And not just because I'd never actually been to Mexico (still haven't). What I wanted to do was write novels. I wanted to write them desperately. It was the only thing I could imagine ever wanting to do. So when September arrived, and the travel guide had gone to press, I bought a car—a 1985 Subaru GL, herb green—and set out west to find somewhere to write them.

At that point in my life I had written a handful of short stories, a much smaller handful of which had been published in college magazines. Sophomore year one of them even won a campus prize. Second prize, but still: I felt like I was ready to step up to the big canvas. I'd never been west of Chicago, but the West seemed like a place where you could lose yourself and hunker down and get some real work done. My plan was to drive till I got to a suitably small town, a dot on a map somewhere, get a job in some unstrenuous service industry, fall in love with the local lonely librarian, and write my books.

Loneliness itself didn't worry me. I genuinely thought that because I wanted to be a writer, I was different from other people: mysterious, self-contained, a lone wolf, Han Solo. I was immune.

I dropped off an already-ex-girlfriend at her parents' house in Queens, then drove on through the industrial countryside of Pennsylvania as it softened in the first autumn rains. I drove all day, no specific destination in mind; I figured I'd know it when I saw it. I'd never done much long-haul driving before. It was harder than I expected: less romantic, more boring.

I listened to the Clarence Thomas hearings on the radio. I ate alone at roadside diners, reading a copy of *Mao II*. One evening I stopped on a roadside embankment to pee and a swarm of crickets leapt up at me out of the grass in a solid wall, which caused me to fall over backward mid-pee. At night I would find an empty field, or a dead-end street, or a neglected parking lot, recline the passenger seat of the Subaru back as far as it would go, and sleep in my car.

What I hadn't counted on, though, was the sheer, dispiriting width of the state of Pennsylvania. It took the fight out of me. While superficially high-functioning, I was in fact easily daunted, and instead of driving west I gave up and veered north to Niagara Falls. If I failed to cross the country I could at least check off one major geographical milestone.

The falls were surrounded by a corona of honeymoon motels that underscored my growing sense of isolation. I had second thoughts about what I was doing. My friends were getting on with their lives, moving to plausible-sounding places like Seattle and Atlanta, starting sensible jobs and graduate schools and professional schools, and what the hell was I doing out here, all by myself? Did I really think I was some kind of novel-writing genius person? I got out of my Subaru and saw the falls and was duly impressed. Then I got back in and headed back east.

But I couldn't go back to Boston, not yet, not when I'd just lit out for the territories so dramatically, so I angled northeast instead, through Adirondack Park and the Vanderwhacker Mountain Wild Forest. It rained harder. I spent another night in the front seat and was awakened by a farmer shooing me out of his field, where I'd parked in the dark. My car wouldn't start, so we walked up to his house together and called a mechanic. The farmer wasn't interested in my voyage of literary self-discovery. He was a sober and pragmatic man. He had actual important work to do. I felt very young and very callow next to him.

So I kept driving. I was clinging to my dream of glorious literary isolation, and it was dawning on me that I could still save it. I could turn my vision of a dusty town in Idaho into a vision of a snug farmhouse in Maine, thoroughly socked in by a deep silent winter. That was the thing for a writer! Having grown up in Massachusetts, I always knew that our winters were a halfhearted, watered-down version of the real thing, the sort of thing they had up north. I thought of *The Outermost House* by Henry Beston. I'd never actually read it, but the title always evoked for me a powerful sense of contemplative isolation. I was going to get me some of that.

I drove through Portland—which was charming but didn't seem northerly or outermost enough—and stopped just short of Bangor—didn't want to overdo it—which left me in Ellsworth, Maine. I bought a copy of a local paper for the real estate listings. Then I parked on a back road, wrapped myself in my overcoat, and got ready to sleep in my car again. A kindly passerby stopped to ask me if I was lost. I told him I knew exactly where I was going. But I didn't know. I can't overstate how little I knew about myself at twenty-two or how little I'd thought about what I was doing. When I graduated from college I genuinely believed that the creative life was the apex of human existence, and that to work at an ordinary office job was a betrayal of that life, and I had to pursue that life at all costs. Management consulting, law school, med school, those were fine for other people—I didn't judge!—but I was an artist. I was special. I was sparkly. I would walk another path. And I would walk it alone. That was another thing I knew about being an artist: you didn't need other people. Other people were a distraction. My little chrysalis of genius was going to seat one and one only.

I found an apartment in Ellsworth, a stubby wing of a farmhouse that the owner had turned into a rental unit, miles out of town on a sparsely developed dirt road. It was perfect except for the bathroom, which was only technically indoors by virtue of a couple of thin sheets of plywood, and which provided no more than sixty consecutive seconds of hot water at a time. But great artists had suffered worse. I moved in, unpacked my belongings, set up my Mac Classic, and got to work.

It was my first experience of writing full-time, and I could do five or six hours a day, but that still left me with a lot of unarable time to dispose of, so I took a lot of walks. I explored the area around the farmhouse. I can still see it with cartographic clarity, from above, like the map of the Hundred Acre Wood in Winnie-the-Pooh. Turn left on the dirt road and you got to a creepy one-room Pentecostal church with boarded-up windows. Turning right took you over a concrete bridge above a little dammed creek, which I used to toss little sticks into. Beyond the bridge and the creek were the empty but surprisingly well-appointed grounds of a summer camp for disturbed teenagers.

When I didn't walk, I drove. I listened to the radio: It was the fall of Prince's "Diamonds and Pearls" and U2's "Mysterious Ways," two perfectly decent songs that through no fault of their own I never ever want to hear again. Back behind a local pharmacy there was a room full of arcade games, and I spent hours in front of an obscure but compelling side-scroller called *Heavy Unit*, in which you piloted a two-dimensional ship armed with lasers and bombs through a hostile and ultimately fatal cavern.

I spent a lot of time at the library too. Though it turned out that none of the librarians were lonely.

But I was lonely. It was the first fall I'd ever spent out of school, and I'd never been that isolated before. Loneliness was a different animal back then. There were no cell phones. There was no texting, no Facebook, no Twitter, no email. Long-distance calls cost money. The web hadn't even been invented yet. I had to get my pornography in the form of magazines. You can still be lonely now, but back then it had a different texture to it. It was raw and uncut and feral.

I did write a lot that fall, but unfortunately I didn't write very well. I'd spent my undergraduate years worshipping the modernists—Joyce, Kafka, Proust, Hemingway, Woolf. I thought that *Mrs. Dalloway* was the most perfect novel of the twentieth century (I still think that). But when I tried to apply their techniques to the topic of my suburban childhood and adolescence, it was pretty slow going. The modernists are easy to admire and tough to imitate. Their particular brand of literary performance is a high-wire act, and if you're not a virtuoso, you're a disaster, and I was not a virtuoso.

I'd also just read Donald Barthelme's *Snow White*, which seemed to me to be the shape of things to come: a bridge to the novel's glorious postmodern future. But when you're trying to write like Donald Barthelme even being a virtuoso isn't good enough. You have to be Donald Barthelme.

On Friday and Saturday nights there was a twenty-three-and-under club in Bangor, forty-five minutes away, and I drove up there a few times, desperate for some human contact. The club was alcohol free, so before I went in I would chug from a fifth of vodka on the passenger seat. But once I got inside, something went wrong. I felt like there was an invisible barrier between me and other people, one that no amount of vodka could dissolve. I had forgotten how to talk to people. I carried around a fair amount of social anxiety already, and all the time I was spending alone had made it much, much worse.

So I would stand around like a lump, shoot some pool in a back room, then drive home alone through fields of cold-stunted pines, no less desperate, while Morrissey sang "How Soon Is Now?" on the Subaru's cassette player.

Money was getting to be a problem. By the end of October I was running through my travel-guide cash pretty fast. I looked for jobs, but there wasn't much out there. Ellsworth was heavily dependent on summer tourism, and it emptied out in the fall. I signed up with temp agencies. I applied for a job as a grounds keeper at a golf club, as an editor at a newspaper in Bar Harbor, as a mailman on rural routes. No one hired me. I was starting to feel a little untouchable.

I did meet a girl, eventually. I've forgotten her name— Jessica, I want to say—but she worked at the local bookstore, which actually sold primarily stationery supplies. I'd dropped off a résumé there, and she called the number on it, not to offer me a job but because she and I were practically the only people in our early twenties in the entire area. We went out for drinks a couple of times and I was very, very grateful for her company, but there was no attraction there whatsoever, on either side. She wasn't over her last boyfriend, who'd moved to Los Angeles to play one of the turtles in the Teenage Mutant Ninja Turtles movie.

At the time I'm not even sure I understood how lonely I was. I had friends back in the real world, but I never asked anyone to visit me. On some level I still didn't believe that I could be lonely, even though it was staring me in the face, all day and all night.

By the end of November my sanity was starting to sag under the weight of all that solitude and empty time and creative
failure. I wrote less and less and liked less and less of what I
wrote. I felt like I couldn't go to bed till I'd accomplished
something, anything, but usually that just meant I stayed up
till dawn and then collapsed from exhaustion. I had no TV, but
I would watch any movie Hollywood cared to release: *Hook*,
Bugsy, *Cape Fear*, *Dead Again*, *Billy Bathgate*, *Star Trek VI: The
Undiscovered Country*, *Highlander II: The Quickening*. Books and
music started to feel unnaturally vivid. I played a Roxette al-
bum (it was *Joyride*) over and over again and analyzed the lyrics
hermeneutically. I read *Ubik*, which did not make my grasp on
reality any firmer. There was a supermarket where you could
buy old comic books by the bale for almost nothing, and I became deeply absorbed in Captain America's search for the Red
Skull (who'd faked his own death, but Cap wasn't buying it).

The weather got colder. The bathroom situation was becoming a problem: showering was a Shackletonian ordeal
punctuated by a brief scalding interlude. I couldn't afford to
keep the rest of the house properly heated either, so I stayed in
bed a lot, drinking Baileys straight from the bottle. The house
began to be plagued by flies that seemed to live in the walls.
They were dormant at night, probably because of the cold,
but when the sun warmed them up they came buzzing out in
hordes, and I spent hours stalking around the apartment swat-
ting them. One night in December, when the temperature
went down to fifteen below, I took off all my clothes and ran
around on the lawn naked just to see what it felt like.

I honestly don't remember much after December. I kept a journal, which is still on my old Mac Classic, but no force on earth could induce me to read it now (though I do remember that I ironically titled it "My Struggle," thus anticipating Karl Ove Knausgaard by a decade and a half). I know I must have written and mailed off applications to a half dozen MFA programs, because the following spring I got back a half dozen rejections. I remember hearing the sonar guitar riff of Nirvana's "Smells Like Teen Spirit" for the first time on New Year's Eve, which I spent glued to the radio, party of one. Sometimes I went to a nearby buffalo farm to watch the buffalo—there were only three of them—huddling together in the cold with an air of disinherited majesty. When things were at their very worst I would go down to the basement.

The guy who owned the farmhouse was a retired schoolteacher, and his hobby was making pickles. The basement was where he kept his pickle barrels, and late at night, when I was at my loneliest and most wretched, I used to jimmy the lock and creep down there. It was cold, and the floor was packed dirt, and there was no light—probably there was a light switch somewhere but I could never find it, so I was in complete darkness. Working by touch I slid the tops off the pickle barrels and felt the half-pickled cucumbers bobbing around in the brine. Then, slowly and methodically, crouching on the dirt floor in the cold and the dark, I ate them.

Maine was trying to teach me something, but I was a slow learner. I was trying to write about what I knew, which in itself probably wasn't a bad idea, but I thought that what I knew about was myself, and on that point I could not have been more wrong. I didn't know the first thing about myself, and there was only so much about myself that being alone could teach me. I went to Maine to face my demons, and turn them into art, but the truth was that I couldn't face them. Not yet, and not alone.

I lived like that for two more months before I called it quits; I lasted six months in all. Not a single word I wrote there was ever published. Afterward I told people I left because I ran out of money, which was objectively true, but it wasn't the real truth. The real truth was that I left because I was sick of being cold and lonely and a lousy writer. I had finally reached the tipping point where the misery of living alone in Maine out-weighed the misery of having to admit to myself that it wasn't working, that I did need other human beings, and that I wasn't a genius after all. I would have admitted anything as long as I didn't have to live in Maine anymore.

When I finally made up my mind to leave Ellsworth, I was so relieved I felt like I was weightless. I couldn't believe it was finally over. I felt like I was walking on the moon. I stayed up all night packing everything I owned into the Subaru and left just as the sky was starting to show cornflower blue on the horizon. I drove out of town—the radio was playing "Tangled Up in Blue." Then I drove back into town when I realized I'd forgotten my one good kitchen knife, retrieved it—terrified that I would somehow be discovered and detained there permanently—and drove back out again, this time for good.

Alone Time

LENA DUNHAM

"I'm going to die alone." It's a refrain often uttered by women, with a kind of tragicomic self-awareness, after a bad date or the breakup of a brief romance or the adoption of a calico cat. I can hardly count the rom-coms that hinge on this premise (a woman has resigned herself to a life of takeout, cheap Chardonnay, and quirky pajamas). But even said jokingly, the words are possessed of a horrible tyranny, as though aloneness is an island on which, as punishment for failing to successfully adapt yourself to romantic love, you are marooned. Alone is a place where nobody would want to go on vacation, much less live permanently.

It was December when we broke up, that kind of confusing weather where glaring sunlight makes the cold air feel even colder. We sat in our shared kitchen of nearly four years and quietly faced each other, acknowledging what nobody wanted to say: That obsessive connection had turned to blind devotion, and the blinders were coming off to reveal that we had evolved separately (the least shocking reason of all and perhaps the most common). That anger wasn't sexy or sustainable.

That our hearts were still broken from trying so hard to fix it but no longer uncertain about whether we could. The finality stunned me, and I remember muttering, "But what if we still went on dates?" He laughed sadly. "Whatever you want."

But we knew there would be no dates, only the kind of loving but overly careful check-ins that define a separation after longtime togetherness, after hundreds upon hundreds of nights curled against each other in bed, after thousands of takeout boxes and millions of text messages and then the side-by-side texting, too, on the couch, under the dim blue light of the TV. Our home, a sprawling loft bought when we brimmed with shared plans for each room, was no longer a space of comfort. And it was hard, in this moment, to summon what it had been, what we had felt, the routines that defined and outlined our life as a couple.

The sound of the washing machine starting up without your having pressed the button, the days you get up first and the days that he does. The hours you lose to shared silence on a Sunday and the back and forth, back and forth to the bodega, taking turns or walking together in jackets either too light or too heavy for the season (nobody in this house is in the habit of checking the weather). It is impossible, in the moment of separation, to access just how valuable each and every one of these mundane acts will seem in a week or a month or four months. You won't lie in your new bed, your solitary bed, thinking of your first date on a rainy night in April or that first *I love you* after drinks at the Carlyle (each of us ordered scotch to impress the other; neither lightweight consumed it). Not the castle on

the beach in Portugal or the ocean in the Maldives full of fish
the color of lipstick. You won't be stuck on the Technicolor
memories but rather the odd, quiet details that proved, again
and again, that you were definitely not alone. We made the
mutual decision that he would keep our home (he's always
loved it fiercely, while I got anxiety in the elevator), and I
would regroup at my parents' place, ten minutes away by cab.

I used to love solitude. I considered it luxurious, a state
in which fantasy and reality mixed and my world took on
the mystical potency of a solstice gathering of nude witches.
For this reason I hated summer camp, where the opportunities
to be alone were scant. By age fourteen I was already pretty
charmed by myself, and living for a month in a bunk of pubes-
cent, writhing female life felt restrictive at best and repulsive
at worst. One day a field trip was planned to a nearby water
park, where we would all wear our green-and-white uniforms
over our bathing suits and be closely watched as we splashed in
the shallow end of a heavily urinated-in public water feature.
No, thank you.

And so I did what any logical adolescent would do: I invented, with perfect symptomatic accuracy, a case of strep
throat. Headache. Pain when swallowing. Vague chills. My
case was airtight. They couldn't question me until they got the
swab back, which could take up to two days. I was quarantined
on a cot in a corner in the nurse's cabin, a place you went only
if something had gone horribly awry. For a few hours she sat at
her desk and I feigned feverish weakness until she announced
that she was headed to lunch and would be back in an hour,

the screen door slamming behind her as she waddled down the hill. And in that moment I realized that, for the first time in weeks, I was alone. The light was bright and dusty. I could feel the wind through the open window, and I released the expression of agony I'd been using as my disguise. I lay perfectly still, almost too delighted.

In high school my bedroom was a temple to personal space, the walls pasted completely with pictures (of Sylvia Plath and Jimmy Fallon, two very different but equally essential formative influences). On the walls I had scrawled images in lipstick of gaunt girls with big mouths and trees with extensive roots, and it never once occurred to me that this might be off-putting, maybe even send up a flare about my mental health. On a prehistoric laptop I typed doleful poems about the solitude I was actually relishing, and when I wasn't inside I was walking in and out of various dollar stores—alone—to pick up crafting supplies (if you've never glued a bunch of plastic grapes to a six-dollar mirror, try it!). My independence was still novel, and every day felt like an opportunity to indulge in my own company, to soak in it like a bubble bath.

Then, at college, came my first serious relationship. He was a beautiful, anxious film student with a blond beard and a red bike. I was in awe of him and quickly installed myself like a light fixture in his bedroom. He was monkish in his sleep patterns, and I stayed up much of the night staring at him: He was here. He was mine. When he moved into an efficiency apartment off campus, he told me he'd like a few nights a week to himself, to "just focus inward." Rather than embrace the solo time, I would sit in my own bedroom, filled with desperate, sickened longing. One night I so convinced myself of the wrongness of our separation that I biked as fast as I could (please picture Miss Gulch in *The Wizard of Oz*, pedaling aggressively to avoid the coming tornado) and landed on his doorstep weeping. He offered me tea and counsel, then sent me home—admirable boundaries—but having had a taste of domesticity, I was almost chemically changed, rewired. The independence I had so prized was replaced with a mourning that could be sated only by consistent male company, even if (as would happen later on with other boys) that company was rude in bars, talked loudly through art-house movies, and made sure to point out my less than ideal breast-to-butt ratio. Anything would do.

Even if some people like to be alone, nobody likes to be lonely. It's been the subject of more art than can be consumed in a lifetime, the human aversion to loneliness and also the way we attune ourselves to it, become entrenched in a routine that isolates us. Too much has been said about the way technology allows us to experience the illusion of connection and retreat further into hermetic patterns, but it bears repeating that texts, emails, Facebook pokes, and Twitter faves do not a social life make. People are, it would seem, lonelier than ever and also less used to being alone.

I recently spent the day with a girlfriend who was ruminating, almost obsessively, on what she would do for dinner that night. "I'm considering going out to eat alone," she said, as if she were confessing to the murder of an innocent family of farmers. I'm not exaggerating when I say that she spent hours upon hours weighing the pros ("I really love the hamburgers at this place") and cons ("But won't it look weird? Maybe not if I sit at the bar").

"You're ridiculous," I said. "I love to eat alone. I live for it. What's more luxurious than enjoying your food without someone talking your freaking ear off?"

But I looked into my recent past and tried to remember such a time—sitting alone in an Indian restaurant spooning paneer onto my plate unmolested, or wearing my summer dress outside a café as I pored over the paper—and I was completely unable to locate an image of it. It was that pesky six-year relationship and the habits of someone unused to venturing out without a companion's prodding. For an exquisite moment, rather than mourn the loss of my partner, I mourned the loss of my bravery. I used to have no problem staring into the face of the hostess when I said, "Just one for dinner, thank you."

As my relationship had unbraided itself, I would often fantasize about my own space, the mythical room of one's own that Virginia Woolf once told every woman writer to demand, and I'd go so far as to conjure a floor plan, place the furnishings down, stack my books. But that was easy to imagine with a living, breathing body beside me, the constant option to call someone and complain about the chaos of my day or the stain on my skirt or the irritatingly apologetic way in which the woman at the pharmacy had asked for two forms of ID. Now, security blanket removed, folded, and shipped to some distant warehouse, I moved in with my parents and lay across their spare bed texting everyone I knew, "sup?"

So how do you get back your taste for solo life, overcome the fear of your own thoughts? Even when my partner was away for work, the house had always been full with his presence—a wayward red sock, a pile of used earplugs. A Batman watch bought on eBay but never worn.

I started slowly, with a bath, the kind that lasts so long you resemble a Shar-Pei, the kind where the water goes from scalding to fairly drinkable, the kind you let drain around your shivering body as you remember moles you'd forgotten dotted your abdomen. I found that the bath was a good starting place because bathing alone is natural, something you might even do when someone in the other room is Skyping their cousin or playing video games.

I read a poetry book cover to cover sitting at the kitchen counter, double-fisting leftover Danish, while my parents were out for the night enjoying a more active social life than I do.

Then I stepped into a restaurant not far from the house and asked for the table by the window, where I ordered only tea and a bread basket but considered it a start.

Finally, four months after the end, I found myself spending a weekend in the country, and I stepped outside and away from my companions, onto a gravel path, and in the dimming pink of the sunset I began along my way. It was simple—one foot in front of the other, hands swinging at my sides—but I thought, rather dramatically, I will remember this moment all my life. I had not, for once, succumbed to the numbing effect

that sleep can have on the grieving. I had not demanded that
my entire family join me in the TV room to rewatch a sitcom.
I had made the choice to face the world—trees, sky, even a
rude, shoe-thieving neighborhood dog named Rico—on my
own, with the power and presence of someone who can tol-
erate herself.

I moved out of my parents' place. My new apartment was
temporary, clean, and corporate, and soon the movers would
stack nearly seventy small boxes, inefficiently but lovingly
packed (a dish between two items of clothing, a trophy crush-
ing a wide-brimmed hat) by the man with whom I once shared
a humming home. I put my hands on my knees, winded from
the sheer marathon of putting up with my own mind, and
looked around. Outside, boats moved along the East River like
my pain meant nothing to them. Someone would be coming
over soon, the electric current of new romance in the air, but I
was still defining myself by what I had lost. And yet, standing
alone in a temporary space, I could still feel the light in the
nurse's cabin bright on my face and the relief of the quiet, my
quiet, to do with as I like, and the expanse of unused time
stretching out before me.

If I were being didactic I would say that this, this pure and
fiery solitude, is the time in which women form themselves—
and that a patriarchal society has removed that privilege from
us through the threat of eternal loneliness as a penance for the
sin of loving yourself.

If I were being poetic I'd say that I felt like Peter Pan, having his shadow sewn back on by an obliging Wendy. I could see

clearly just how much work I had to do to move forward, how it was almost like picking up a second job to make emotional ends meet. My new pastime was making the quiet all right for myself, defining my boundaries so that I had space to dream. I made a list, on actual paper, of things I like to do, activities that bring me joy, pursuits that nourish me. (The ground rules: Do not mention work, work dinners, or masturbation. This is purely a list of useless but fulfilling stuff, like beading.)

Friends called and I started to feel like I could pick up without worrying about the hitch in my chest the moment they asked, "How are you feeling about it all?" I had some answers now that they might actually buy, that sounded healthy and self-assured and like the woman of extreme independence I wanted to become again. "I'm good, just chugging along." But if I were being honest I'd answer them by saying that my heart could still ache for one home as I returned to myself in another.

To Speak Is to Blunder but I Venture

YIYUN LI

In a dream the other night, I was back in Beijing, at the entrance of my family's apartment complex, where a public telephone, a black rotary, had once been guarded by the old women from the neighborhood association. They used to listen without hiding their disdain or curiosity while I was on the phone with friends; when I finished, they would complain about the length of the conversation before logging it into their book and calculating the charge. In those days, I accumulated many errands before I went to use the telephone, lest my parents notice my extended absence. My allowance—which was what I could scrimp and save from my lunch money—was spent on phone calls and stamps and envelopes. Like a character in a Victorian novel, I checked our mail before my parents did and collected letters to me from friends before my parents could intercept them.

In my dream, I asked for the phone. Two women came out of a front office. I recognized them: in real life, they are both gone. No, they said; the service is no longer offered, because everyone has a cell phone these days. There was nothing extraordinary about the dream—a melancholy visit to the past in this manner is beyond one's control—but for the fact that the women spoke to me in English.

Years ago, when I started writing in English, my husband asked if I understood the implication of the decision. What he meant was not the practical concerns, though there were plenty: the nebulous hope of getting published; the lack of a career path as had been laid out for me in science, my first field of postgraduate study in America; the harsher immigration regulation I would face as a fiction writer. Many of my college classmates from China, as scientists, acquired their green cards under a national interest waiver. An artist is not of much importance to any nation's interest.

My husband, who writes computer programs, was asking about language. Did I understand what it meant to renounce my mother tongue?

Nabokov once answered a question he must have been tired of being asked: "My private tragedy, which cannot, indeed should not, be anybody's concern, is that I had to abandon my natural language, my natural idiom." That something is called a tragedy, however, means it is no longer personal. One weeps out of private pain, but only when the audience swarms in and claims understanding and empathy do people call it a tragedy. One's grief belongs to oneself; one's tragedy, to others.

I often feel a tinge of guilt when I imagine Nabokov's woe. Like all intimacies, the intimacy between one and one's mother tongue can be comforting and irreplaceable, yet it can also demand more than what one is willing to give, or more than one is capable of giving. If I allow myself to be honest, my private salvation, which cannot and should not be anybody's concern, is that I disowned my native language.

In the summer and autumn of 2012, I was hospitalized in California and in New York for suicide attempts, the first time for a few days and the second time for three weeks. During those months, my dreams often took me back to Beijing. I would be standing on top of a building—one of those gray, Soviet-style apartment complexes—or I would be lost on a bus traveling through an unfamiliar neighborhood. Waking up, I would list in my journal images that did not appear in my dreams: a swallow's nest underneath a balcony, the barbed wires at the rooftop, the garden where old people sat and ex-changed gossip, the mailboxes at street corners—round, green, covered by dust, with handwritten collection times behind a square window of half-opaque plastic.

Yet I have never dreamed of Iowa City, where I first landed in America, in 1996, at the age of twenty-three. When asked about my initial impression of the place, I cannot excavate anything from memory to form a meaningful answer. During a recent trip there from my home in California, I visited a neighborhood that I used to walk through every day. The one-story houses, which were painted in pleasantly muted col-ors, with gardens in the front enclosed by white picket fences, had not changed. I realized that I had never described them to others or to myself in Chinese, and when English was estab-lished as my language they had become everyday mundanities.

What happened during my transition from one language to another did not become memory.

People often ask about my decision to write in English. The switch from one language to another feels natural to me, I reply, though that does not say much, just as one can hardly give a convincing explanation as to why someone's hair turns gray on one day but not on another. But this is an inane analogy, I realize, because I do not want to touch the heart of the matter. Yes, there is something unnatural, which I have refused to accept. Not the fact of writing in a second language—there are always Nabokov and Conrad as references, and many of my contemporaries as well—or that I impulsively gave up a reliable career for writing. It's the absoluteness of my abandonment of Chinese, undertaken with such determination that it is a kind of suicide.

The tragedy of Nabokov's loss is that his misfortune was easily explained by public history. His story—of being driven by a revolution into permanent exile—became the possession of other people. My decision to write in English has also been explained as a flight from my country's history. But unlike Nabokov, who had been a published Russian writer, I never wrote in Chinese. Still, one cannot avoid the fact that a private decision, once seen through a public prism, becomes a metaphor. Once, a poet of Eastern European origin and I—we both have lived in America for years, and we both write in English—were asked to read our work in our native languages at a gala. But I don't write in Chinese, I explained, and the organizer apologized for her misunderstanding. I offered to read Li Po or Du Fu or any of the ancient poets I had grown up memorizing, but instead it was arranged for me to read poetry by a political prisoner.

A metaphor's desire to transcend diminishes any human story; its ambition to illuminate blinds those who create metaphors. In my distrust of metaphors I feel a kinship with George Eliot: "We all of us, grave or light, get our thoughts entangled in metaphors, and act fatally on the strength of them." My abandonment of my first language is personal, so deeply personal that I resist any interpretation—political or historical or ethnographical. This, I know, is what my husband was questioning years ago: Was I prepared to be turned into a symbol by well-intentioned or hostile minds?

Chinese immigrants of my generation in America criticize my English for not being native enough. A compatriot, after reading my work, pointed out, in an email, how my language is neither lavish nor lyrical, as a real writer's language should be: *You write only simple things in simple English, you should be ashamed of yourself*, he wrote in a fury. A professor—an American writer—in graduate school told me that I should stop writing, as English would remain a foreign language to me. Their concerns about ownership of a language, rather than making me as impatient as Nabokov, allow me secret laughter. English is to me as random a choice as any other language. What one goes toward is less definitive than that from which one turns away.

Before I left China, I destroyed the journal that I had kept for years and most of the letters written to me, those same letters I had once watched out for, lest my mother discover them.

Those that I could not bring myself to destroy I sealed up and brought with me to America, though I will never open them again. My letters to others I would have destroyed, too, had I had them. These records, of the days I had lived time and time over, became intolerable now that my time in China was over. But this violent desire to erase a life in a native language is only wishful thinking. One's relationship with the native language is similar to that with the past. Rarely does a story start where we wish it had or end where we wish it would.

One crosses the border to become a new person. One finishes a manuscript and cuts off the characters. One adopts a language. These are false and forced frameworks, providing illusory freedom, as time provides illusory leniency when we, in anguish, let it pass monotonously. "To kill time," an English phrase that still chills me: time can be killed but only by frivolous matters and purposeless activities. No one thinks of suicide as a courageous endeavor to kill time.

During my second hospital stay, in New York, a group of nursing students came to play bingo one Friday night. A young woman, another patient, asked if I would join her. Bingo, I said, I've never in my life played that. She pondered for a moment, and said that she had played bingo only in the hospital. It was her eighth hospitalization when I met her; she had taken middle school courses for a while in the hospital, when she was younger, and, once, she pointed out a small patch of fenced-in green where she and other children had been let out for exercise. Her father often visited her in the afternoon, and I would watch them sitting together playing a game, not attempting a conversation. By then, all words must have been inadequate, language doing little to help a mind survive time.

Yet language is capable of sinking a mind. One's thoughts are slavishly bound to language. I used to think that an abyss is a moment of despair becoming interminable; but any moment, even the direst, is bound to end. What's abysmal is that one's erratic language closes in on one like quicksand: "You are nothing. You must do anything you can to get rid of this nothingness." We can kill time, but language kills us.

Patient reports feeling . . . like she is a burden to her loved ones— much later, I read the notes from the emergency room. I did not have any recollection of the conversation. A burden to her loved ones: this language must have been provided to me. I would never use the phrase in my thinking or my writing. But my resistance has little to do with avoiding a platitude. To say "a burden" is to grant oneself weight in other people's lives; to call them "loved ones" is to fake one's ability to love. One does not always want to be subject to self-interrogation imposed by a cliché.

When Katherine Mansfield was still a teenager, she wrote in her journal about a man next door playing "Swanee River" on a cornet, for what seemed like weeks. "I wake up with the 'Swannee River,' eat it with every meal I take, and go to bed eventually with 'all de world am sad and weary' as a lullaby." I read Mansfield's notebooks and Marianne Moore's letters around the same time, when I returned home from New York. In a letter, Moore described a night of fund-raising at Bryn Mawr. Maidens in bathing suits and green bathing tails on a raft: "It was Really most realistic . . . way down upon the Swanee River."

"How do you feel about staying in power?"

I marked the entries because they reminded me of a moment I had forgotten. I was nine, and my sister thirteen. On a Saturday afternoon, I was in our apartment and she was on the balcony. My sister had joined the middle school choir that year, and in the autumn sunshine she sang in a voice that was beginning to leave girlhood. "Way down upon the Swanee River. Far, far away. That's where my heart is turning ever; that's where the old folks stay."

The lyrics were translated into Chinese. The memory, too, should be in Chinese. But I cannot see our tiny garden with the grapevine, which our father cultivated and which was later uprooted by our wrathful mother, or the bamboo fence dotted with morning glories, or the junk that occupied half the balcony—years of accumulations piled high by our hoarder father—if I do not name these things to myself in English. I cannot see my sister, but I can hear her sing the lyrics in English. I can seek to understand my mother's vulnerability and cruelty, but language is the barrier I have chosen. "Do you know, the moment I die your father will marry someone else?" my mother used to whisper to me when I was little. "Do you know that I cannot die, because I don't want you to live under a stepmother?" Or else, taken over by inexplicable rage, she would say that I, the only person she had loved, deserved the ugliest death because I did not display enough gratitude. But I have given these moments—what's possible to be put into English—to my characters. Memories, left untranslated, can be disowned; memories untranslatable can become someone else's story.

Over the years, my brain has banished Chinese. I dream in English. I talk to myself in English. And memories—not only those about America but also those about China; not only those carried with me but also those archived with the wish to forget—are sorted in English. To be orphaned from my native language felt, and still feels, like a crucial decision.

When we enter a world—a new country, a new school, a party, a family or class reunion, an army camp, a hospital—we speak the language it requires. The wisdom to adapt is the wisdom to have two languages: the one spoken to others and the one spoken to oneself. One learns to master the public language not much differently from the way that one acquires a second language: assess the situations, construct sentences with the right words and the correct syntax, catch a mistake if one can avoid it, or else apologize and learn the lesson after a blunder. Fluency in the public language, like fluency in a second language, can be achieved with enough practice.

Perhaps the line between the two is, and should be, fluid; it is never so for me. I often forget, when I write, that English is also used by others. English is my private language. Every word has to be pondered before it becomes a word. I have no doubt—can this be an illusion?—that the conversation I have with myself, however linguistically flawed, is the conversation that I have always wanted, in the exact way I want it to be.

In my relationship with English, in this relationship with the intrinsic distance between a nonnative speaker and an adopted language that makes people look askance, I feel invisible but not estranged. It is the position I believe I always want in life. But with every pursuit there is the danger of crossing a line, from invisibility to erasure.

There was a time when I could write well in Chinese. In school, my essays were used as models; in the army, where I spent a year of involuntary service between the ages of eighteen and nineteen, our squad leader gave me the choice between drafting a speech for her and cleaning the toilets or the pigsties—I always chose to write. Once, in high school, I entered an oratory contest. Onstage, I saw that many of the listeners were moved to tears by the poetic and insincere lies I had made up; I moved myself to tears, too. It crossed my mind that I could become a successful propaganda writer. I was disturbed by this. A young person wants to be true to herself and to the world. But it did not occur to me to ask, Can one's intelligence rely entirely on the public language; can one form a precise thought, recall an accurate memory, or even feel a genuine feeling, with only the public language?

My mother, who loves to sing, often sings the songs from her childhood and youth, many of them words of propaganda from the 1950s and '60s. But there is one song she has reminisced about all her life because she does not know how to sing it. She learned the song in kindergarten, the year Communism took over her hometown; she can remember only the opening line.

There was an old woman in the hospital in New York who

sat in the hallway with a pair of shiny red shoes. "I feel like Dorothy," she said as she showed me the shoes, which she had chosen from the donations to patients. Some days, her mind was lucid, and she would talk about the red shoes that hurt her feet but which she could not part with or the medication that made her brain feel dead and left her body in pain. Other days, she talked to the air, an endless conversation with the unseen. People who had abandoned her by going away or dying returned and made her weep.

I often sat next to this lonesome Dorothy. Was I eavesdropping? Perhaps, but her conversation was beyond encroachment. That one could reach a point where the border between public and private language no longer matters is frightening. Much of what one does—to avoid suffering, to seek happiness, to stay healthy—is to keep a safe space for one's private language. Those who have lost that space have only one language left. My grandmother, according to my mother and her siblings, had become a woman who talked to the unseen before she was sent to the asylum to die. There's so much to give up: hope, freedom, dignity. A private language, however, defies any confinement. Death alone can take it away.

Mansfield spoke of her habit of keeping a journal as "being garrulous . . . I must say nothing affords me the same relief." Several times, she directly addressed the readers—her posterity—in a taunting manner, as though laughing at them for taking her dead words seriously. I would prefer to distrust her. But it would be dishonest not to acknowledge the solace of reading her words. It was in the immediate weeks after the second hospitalization. My life was on hold. There were diagnoses to grapple with, medications to take, protocols to implement, hospital staff to report to, but they were there only to eliminate an option. What to replace it with I could not see, but I knew it was not within anyone's capacity to answer that. Not having the exact language for the bleakness I felt, I devoured Mansfield's words like thirst-quenching poison. Is it possible that one can be held hostage by someone else's words? What I underlined and reread: Are they her thoughts or mine?

"There is naught to do but WORK, but how can I work when this awful weakness makes even the pen like a walking stick?"

"There is something profound & terrible in this eternal desire to establish contact."

"It is astonishing how violently a big branch shakes when a silly little bird has left it. I expect the bird knows it and feels immensely arrogant."

"One only wants to feel sure of another. That's all."

"I realise my faults better than anyone else could realise them. I know exactly where I fail."

"Have people, apart from those far away people, ever existed for me? Or have they always failed me, and faded because I denied them reality? Supposing I were to die, as I sit at this table, playing with my indian paper knife—what would be the difference. No difference at all. Then why don't I commit suicide?"

When one thinks in an adopted language, one arranges and rearranges words that are neutral, indifferent even.

When one remembers in an adopted language, there is a

dividing line in that remembrance. What came before could be someone else's life; it might as well be fiction.

What language, I wonder, does one use to feel? Or does one need a language to feel? In the hospital in New York, one of my doctors asked me to visit a class studying minds and brains. Two medical students interviewed me, following a script. The doctor who led the class, impatient with their tentativeness, sent them back to their seats and posed questions more pointed and unrelenting. To answer him, I had to navigate my thoughts, and I watched him and his students closely, as I was being watched. When he asked about feelings, I said it was beyond my ability to describe what might as well be indescribable.

"If you can be articulate about your thoughts, why can't you articulate your feelings?" the doctor asked.

It took me a year to figure out the answer. It is hard to feel in an adopted language, yet it is impossible in my native language.

Often I think that writing is a futile effort; so is reading; so is living. Loneliness is the inability to speak with another in one's private language. That emptiness is filled with public language or romanticized connections.

After the dream of the public telephone, I remembered a moment in the army. It was New Year's Eve, and we were ordered to watch the official celebration on CCTV. Halfway through the program, a girl on duty came and said that there was a long-distance call for me.

It was the same type of black rotary phone as we had back at the apartment complex, and my sister was on the line. It was the first long-distance call I had received in my life, and the next time would be four years later, back in Beijing, when an American professor phoned to interview me. I still remember the woman, calling from Mount Sinai Hospital in New York City, asking questions about my interests in immunology, talking about her research projects and life in America. My English was good enough to understand half of what she said, and the scratching noises in the background made me sweat for the missed half.

What did my sister and I talk about on that New Year's Eve? In abandoning my native language, I have erased myself from that memory. But erasing, I have learned, does not stop with a new language, and that, my friend, is my sorrow and my selfishness. In speaking and in writing in an adopted language, I have not stopped erasing. I have crossed the line, too, from erasing myself to erasing others. I am not the only casualty in this war against myself.

In an ideal world, I would prefer to have my mind reserved for thinking, and thinking alone. I dread the moment when a thought trails off and a feeling starts, when one faces the eternal challenge of eluding the void for which one does not have words. To speak when one cannot is to blunder. I have spoken by having written—this piece or any piece—for myself and against myself. The solace is with the language I chose. The grief, to have spoken at all.

Am I Still Here?

ANTHONY DOERR

I harbor a dark twin inside. He's a sun-starved, ropy bastard and he lives somewhere north of my heart. Every day he gets a little stronger. He's a weed; he's a creeper; he's a series of thickening wires inside my skull.

Call him Z. I like weather; Z survives in spite of it. I like skiing; Z likes surfing the web. I like looking at trees; Z likes reading news feeds. I pull weeds in the garden; Z whispers in my ear about climate change, nuclear proliferation, ballooning health insurance premiums.

Last week I flew into central Idaho on a ten-seat Britten-Norman Islander to spend five days in the wilderness. The plane's engines throbbed exactly like a heartbeat. The sky was a depthless blue. Little white clouds were reefed on the horizon. Slowly, steadily, the airplane pulled us farther and farther from the gravel airstrip where we started, over the Frank Church Wilderness, over the Soldier Lakes, aquamarine lozenges gleaming in basins, flanked by huge, shattered faces of granite, a hundred miles from anything, and the ridgelines scrolling beneath my window were steadily lulling me into

an intoxication, a daze—the splendor of all this!—and then
Z tapped me (metaphorically) on the (metaphorical) shoulder.

Hey, he said. You haven't checked your email today.

"I think," Thoreau wrote in his essay "Walking," "that I cannot preserve my health and spirits unless I spend four hours a
day at least—and it is commonly more than that—sauntering
through the woods and over the hills and fields absolutely free
from all worldly engagements."

Ha! Four hours! Clearly Thoreau did not own a smartphone.

Yesterday—and this is embarrassing—I checked my email
before leaving for work and after I got to work, and I checked
it every now and then during the day at work, and, after bicy-
cling home from work, a total distance of two miles, I checked
my email again. Just in case a few emails flew over my head
through the rain while I pedaled home.

It's disconcerting, it's shameful. I tell myself email is
work-related. Email is work-related and anything work-
related is family-related, right? Because work makes money
and money feeds the family. Money justifies all. Doesn't it?

What my evil twin Z knows, and what I am loathe to articulate, to even contemplate, is that checking email or tinker-
ing around on Facebook or reading snippets about Politician A
on Blog B is not about making money at all but about asking
the world a very urgent question.

That question is: Am I still here?

Each time Z makes me guide the little mouse cursor to the

Send and Receive buttons, he's hollering into the impossibly complex snarl of underground and aboveground fiber linking every computer to every other: Am I part of this? Am I still here?

Yes, you're here, Z, says Eddie Sloan re: Enlarge Your Penis 3+ Inches (100% GUARANTEED). You're a part of it.

Yes, you're here, Z, says Mark J. Silverman from legal, you're here. Now forward me that memo.

Yes, you're here, Z, says Matt Torrington from requisitions. You're here all right, right here in last place in our football pool.

Since purchasing a little glassy machine called an iPhone, I've started checking email in classrooms and in coffee shops. I've read news articles at stoplights, at my sons' swimming lessons, at restaurants, and yes, once or twice in the bathroom while I peed.

Tap, tap, tap. Scroll, scroll, scroll. Paul Krugman, baseball scores, tide tables, www.edge.org, Immanuel Kant, blender-eats-camcorder, the tour schedule has changed, click here to watch a venomous snail paralyze a goldfish. Information, information, information—it's all sustenance for that raw-boned, insatiable, up-to-the-second twin of mine. I can stand in a river with my little sons beside me pitching pebbles into a deep, brilliant green pool with a flock of geese flapping along overhead and the autumn sun transforming the cottonwoods into an absolute frenzy of color—each leaf a shining, blessed fountain of light—and Z will start whispering in my ear about oil prices, presidential politics, the NFL.

What, Z wants to know, are we missing right *now*?

Addiction, neurologists say, changes the physical shape of our brains. Each time old Z finds another text message, another headline, another update, my brain injects a little dopamine into a reward pathway, and the whole system gets a little bit stronger.

The new-email chime dings on my laptop and—whoosh!—here comes a shot of dopamine.

I feel stronger, says Z.

Five minutes pass, the dopamine fades.

I'm weak, hisses Z. I'm hungry. I need to see a picture of Joe Biden.

What if, while you read the last few paragraphs, something in the world has changed? What if, during the past five minutes, someone, somewhere, sent you a text? Shouldn't you go and check?

Being addicted to the wired universe might be perfectly healthy, of course, and it's certainly defensible beneath the triumvirate of technology, curiosity, and progress. I'm the first to admit that there's something enchanting and invigorating about my computer. There's magic in reading a note from a friend in Rome and clicking through Halloween pictures from New Jersey and verifying John Steinbeck's birth date in two clicks. The internet is indeed its own strange, blessed fountain of light.

But sometimes I think Z's demand to feel connected is tilting us both toward derangement, especially when we rise together at 3:00 a.m. and stare for a half hour into the black vacuum of the backyard and drink a cup of tea in the doorway of the kitchen before walking over to the computer and waking it up and finding out that while we sweated and twisted in the bedsheets, BeachReady Body had been preparing a totally unique and groundbreaking Body Transformation Formula for us, as well as for Leslie in New Mexico and Ben in Des Moines.

"We fall in love, we drink hard, we run to and fro upon the earth like frightened sheep," wrote Robert Louis Stevenson. "And now you are to ask yourself if, when all is done, you would not have been better to sit by the fire at home, and be happy thinking."

Do we like sitting by the fire? We do.

Does it make us happy to think? It does. For a while. But pretty soon don't we start worrying, now that we've stepped away from the world, that the world is slipping past without us? Don't we wonder, when we come back: Am I still here?

Oh, the strange mix of revulsion and pleasure Z and I felt when we returned from five days under the sky in the middle of Idaho and watched the email counter piling up: 21, 32, 58, 74 emails! Z has 74 emails! Z is indeed part of it all! Z was missed! Z exists!

We're not the first to wonder about all this, me and Z, not the first to sense that maybe our shared life is rushing by too quickly, too feverishly. We're not the first to feel as if we are scrambling to make our voices heard against an infinite and obliterating silence.

During the five days Z and I spent in the mountains, we saw lots of Shoshone pictographs, paintings made in caves mostly, and under overhangs: finger-painted elk and owls and dogs and triangle-bodied hunters with bows. Many of the pictographs in that area include hash marks, like rows of fence posts scratched downhill, but it's anyone's guess as to what these marks originally meant. Maybe they represented offerings to the spirit world, tallied successful hunts, or recorded vision quests. Maybe they were the consequence of someone sitting beside a fire and thinking happily away.

Whatever they once meant, they mean something else now. They mean memories are fragile, beliefs are tenuous, contexts are temporary. They mean nothing is stable—not mountains, not species, not cultures, not emails. The only quantities that ultimately persist are gravity and mystery. Uproar, as Keats said, is our only music.

What did I do today that will still retain its original meaning two hundred years from now? Might it be better, and more lasting, merely to walk home right now, open the backyard gate, and lie down in the grass?

When was the last time you were dazzled? When was the last time you lay down on a block of granite and fell asleep beneath the sky? Our few remaining pockets of unconnected, unwired time—walks, airplane trips, camp-outs, reading a novel on a beach—are dwindling fast. And yet: The earth is 4.5 billion years old! There are at least 100 billion stars in our galaxy! What could be wrong with shutting down the computer some afternoon and sauntering for four hours through the woods and over the hills and fields?

"Dad!" calls my four-year-old son Owen. He runs inside; his hands are cupped; his eyes are wide open.

"I found a grasshopper leg!" He flexes it back and forth; he wants to know if he can keep it.

I throw my phone onto the couch. I lift my son into my lap.

"When I am in the country," wrote the old English critic William Hazlitt, "I wish to vegetate like the country."

Z hates vegetating. Z wants LinkedIn, Twitter, Google. Z wants me to pick up my phone and finish reading my email. Instead I take my sons on a walk. Clouds are blowing into the valley, big and dark and full of shoulders, and the light is low and golden. The sage, blooming in the gulch beneath our house, billows and shines.

We try to be quiet; we try to be diligent; we try to breathe.

Am I still here?

All I have to do is look into the eyes of my children, walking beside me through the evening.

Yes, Daddy, their eyes say.

Of course you're here, Daddy. You're right here.

A Strange and Difficult Joy

HELENA FITZGERALD

I am terrible at sharing the bed. When my husband is out of town, my first thought is how much space I will get to take up in the bed while he's gone. I know people who claim to sleep on their same side when their partners are gone, the place reserved for the body of their loved one like the seat at the table for Elijah; this has never been and will never be me. I sleep with my limbs giddily starfished across as much of the bed as possible, a self-aggrandizing compass reaching for the edges of the map. When my husband comes home, I'm happy to see him and I also miss the whole space of the bed. I return his half to him grudgingly, making no secret of how I prefer sleeping alone.

The night I moved into an apartment by myself for the first time, I unpacked boxes and ordered a pizza. When the pizza arrived, I was jolted back to a particular suburban memory. In middle school, my parents would go out for date night and leave me in the house by myself with instructions to order a pizza for dinner. The sound of the door closing when they left signaled freedom; I was entirely alone.

I never did anything transgressive or even interesting on those nights—I'd watch a movie and probably fall asleep on the couch. It was about the solitude: the lack of obligation to arrange my face in a way that someone else would understand. Even at age twelve, I understood the weight of that burden, and the relief of its absence. It was the banality of those nights I longed for, doing nothing but doing it completely alone. I imagined adulthood would be a long night like this, ordering a pizza in an empty house—forever.

I was an only child and a lonely kid, which meant I spent a lot of time alone reading books. Classical literature was full of heroes—the vast majority of them were men—who were heroic because they went on solitary quests. The quest narrative was one in which a man whittled away from himself all societal bonds and then, having perfected himself through the crucible of loneliness, returned triumphant to society. Coming-of-age narratives often told stories about men setting out into the elements and learning to survive without help from anyone else; men who wandered on the road far from home and society, learning to fight, and learning when to trust strangers. *The Odyssey* and stories that imitated it followed a man who over the course of adventure and tragedy loses all his companions and his ties to society and has to find his way back through dangers, alone. When these men at last returned from their heroic wanderings, society was still there waiting for them because it had been tended by women. Women never seemed to get the chance to be alone in this same way, were rarely if ever offered the same chance to break free of society, go find themselves, and return a hero.

In popular culture we have "the bachelor pad" and "the bachelor lifestyle" but no such phrases for women. Women who remain alone are objects of fear or pity, witches in the forest or *Cathy* comics. Even the current cultural popularity of female friendship still speaks to how unwilling we are to accept women without a social framework; a woman who is "alone" is a woman who's having brunch with a bunch of other women. When a woman is truly alone, it is the result of a crisis—she is grieving, she has failed to find a partner or a family, she is a problem to be fixed. The family, that fundamental social unit, is traditionally associated with women's obligations. Women are the anchors of social labor, the glue pulling the family, and then the community, together with small talk and good manners and social niceties. Living alone as a woman is not just a luxury but a refusal to bend into the shape of patriarchal assumption and expectation.

When I worked as a tutor to students at European boarding schools, my job often necessitated long-term travel to the cities where my students lived. Traveling for work meant I spent a lot of time in train stations and airports. Sites of arrival and departure are also sites of relationship: couples parting and reuniting; families reassembling or splitting apart; one person breaking from or returning to the unit like a high school math problem about relational distance, the trajectories of two objects, mapped with dotted lines, always returning to each other. I moved through these scenes like a ghost, yet I felt astoundingly whole. I wasn't alone because I had aimed at being with someone and missed—the way women are often portrayed—but because I had aimed squarely at being alone and hit the target.

I lived in Barcelona on my own for a handful of months. My apartment was up seven flights of stairs in an old, strange building, its lobby and staircase as huge and dilapidated as an abandoned opera hall, all flaking opulence and rubbed-off gold paint. My job meant I kept weird hours, and the city kept them with me. More than once I began to make friends, to find myself invited into a group of people. But I never pursued those friendships. Being alone felt like a project to which I had to commit all of myself.

I took long walks around the city, often leaving my phone in my apartment and getting lost on purpose. I eavesdropped strenuously on conversations in bars and coffee shops, piecing together the gaps within a language I was still learning, trying to tune my ear to pronouns and verb tenses. I listened to strangers flirting, their bodies moving in and out of each other's space. I listened to drink orders and laughter spilling out of restaurants at the end of the night. I listened to everything but myself. I allowed myself to turn from participant to spectator. Like the hero in the stories I had read as a kid, I placed myself adjacent to but outside of society and began to understand its workings when I stopped trying to fit myself into it. I faded into the background; it was an enormous relief to not want anything from anyone, to not worry about whether I could persuade anyone to love me.

My apartment's terrace was nestled among nearby buildings within a network of laundry lines and chimneys and picnic tables, struggling roof gardens and barbecues and outdoor parties, an open-faced warren of other people's lives. I watched humanity swarm and choose itself again and again, the couplings and groupings that sutured people together. I stayed apart from it, aware that this time alone was a piece of wild luck, a limited offer. This much solitude was not sustainable, yet part of me wished it could be.

When that job ended and I went back home, I decided to prioritize living by myself. Living alone, especially in a city like New York, is a massive privilege; I was extremely lucky to just barely be able to afford to do so, and during the time when I lived alone, I was never for one single second not worried about money. But I wanted to extend and lean into the lessons I had learned in the months I had been lucky enough to spend alone. My life had been sort of a mess before that; obsessed with pleasing other people and with their reactions to me, I had rarely stopped to take care of myself, and that inability to distinguish between my own needs and those of others had often made me unable to be a caring friend or partner and had left my own life messy and haphazard. There was something deliberate about being alone, something I suspected would allow me to pull together those loose threads, to arrange my life into a shape other than accidental or desperate.

I moved into a small studio apartment and began the slow,

stubborn, unglamorous work of putting my life together, alone. Because I couldn't rely on or blame anyone else in a space I did not share, I learned to call myself out on my bad habits and take responsibility for my own choices and their consequences. I cleaned my apartment when no one was coming over and cooked elaborate meals with no guests in mind but myself. I began to learn to say no to things, to define space for myself. I considered decisions longer and hurt people less. I finally taught myself to establish the boundaries I had never learned to set with others or with myself. With no one else's needs into which to escape, it becomes much more difficult to skid through life on self-delusion and comfortable ignorance. There was nowhere else to go but myself, and no one else available to blame. Being alone calmed the noise that had always crowded into my head, and it allowed me to be both kinder and more accountable.

This rigorous consideration of self was the privilege offered by extended periods of time alone, a privilege that few people, women in particular, are lucky enough to access, and one we are often told represents a failure. I experienced it not as a failure but as a strange and difficult joy. Living alone is a confrontation with the mirror, a removal, if only for certain hours of the day, from the social contract, outside the systems of manners that grow up around women like strangling vines. It is becoming the witch in the forest, powerful and watchful and silent, setting visitors on edge.

●

I had been living alone for a year and a half when my then boyfriend and I decided to move in together. From early on, I knew that what we were doing was something serious, and it made me happy and anxious at the same time. There was a tumbling sense of inevitability, a dread of permanence, at the bottom of my stomach. When I looked directly at our relationship, I had to admit that I wanted to come home to this person every day. But I also wanted to come home to myself.

The idea that we should progress in a clear trajectory from single unit to coupled form, and achieve a sort of emotional success by doing so, seems entirely wrong to me. It is true that living with a partner, when it's truly good, is easier in almost every way, from the lessons in forgiveness, to the heap of congratulations society offers traditional couples, to the very literal material benefits of combining resources and splitting bills. Yet love is also about what we give up when we choose to knit our life into someone else's—to make a home, to share a bed, to inhabit a space together. Being alone is not the terror we escape; it is the reward we give up when we believe something else to be worth the sacrifice. A paired life is not an aspirational state; for me, it is a compromise. With my husband, the world seems less relentless, more forgiving, with fewer teeth and trapdoors. We thread ourselves through each other's difficulties, making the jagged edges of each day cohere. But this coherence, the warmth and support of this relationship, comes at the cost of something else I love almost as much: being alone.

I once thought people entered into relationships to hide from themselves, to burrow into an obsession with another person and escape the facts of their shortcomings. Yet for me, loving someone else, and joining my life with his, required me to sit down with the brutal facts of myself, to sift finely between what is true and what I wish were true, in order to understand what I need and what I can offer. This partnership has been a stark accounting of myself, a wiping away of excuses and avoidances. In this way, its lessons were similar to the lessons I learned from being alone with myself.

I have learned that love, in its closed circuit, can be as antisocial as staying home alone and not speaking aloud to anyone for days. At its best, love turns its face away from good manners, proves itself the opposite of small talk. I have been surprised by how many of the lessons are transferrable, how living together demands the same confrontation with the mirror that living alone did.

But there are so many things I miss about living alone. Many of those things—staying up as late as I want, eating what and when I want, sleeping sprawled sideways across the bed—could be seen as childish, a state of being in which I was never obligated to consider anyone's needs other than my own. Women are pushed out of childhood so quickly, shoved without ceremony into the heavy social obligations of adulthood. Living alone is a reminder that we can make our bodies antisocial, hoarding our selfishness and our silence. Living alone offers the strange and rich pleasures of the world beyond the social, beyond the structures of home and family. Choosing the domestic actively, out of love, is a sacrifice that for me, and for many people, is worth making, but it is still a sacrifice.

While I am happy with my choice to live with my husband, I know that choice follows a narrative approved by forces larger and less benevolent than myself, a narrative I am not happy to know I perpetuate.

Living alone as a woman takes on outsize significance because it offers the right to a full self, one obligated neither to family nor to love. Because we are often denied this fully formed and selfish reckoning, it is difficult to give it up after finding a way into it. There is a mourning in that letting go, as though I am not passing naturally from one stage of maturation to the next but shedding something rarer and more precious. No matter how committed I am to the life I'm building with the person I love, some part of me reaches back to the fierce joy of being alone.

75 x 2

MAILE MELOY

My grandparents were married for seventy-five years, which isn't easy to do. You have to marry young, live a long time, and like the person you're with. Seventy-five years is longer, probably, than people are supposed to be married. Toward the end, it started to feel like a sociology experiment with a tiny sample, or like two people stuck together in a small and leaking lifeboat.

They met in college in Detroit—he bought a car for twenty-five dollars so he could offer her a ride home—and married in 1942, because he was going to war. Lou was nineteen, and Ed was twenty-three, and she took the train by herself across the country to join him in California. He did two tours of duty as a Marine Corps pilot in the Second World War and another two in Korea. They had five children, nine grandchildren, and nine great-grandchildren, and she sewed clothes for most of them and sang them all to sleep. When I was five, I asked her what she'd wanted to be when she grew up, and she said, "I wanted to be a mother. When I was little, I didn't know girls could be anything else."

They moved to Oregon when Ed retired, and she loved to hike. She was generous and gregarious, and competitive at games, and drew people in. In pictures, she is always laughing. Her black hair went white early, and she wore it Jean Seberg–short. On her ninety-second birthday, she was rereading *The Age of Innocence* and still had perfect posture. But after that, the wear began to show. Both she and Ed started forgetting more, and thinking the other had forgotten something, when often they just hadn't heard it. When Lou was most frustrated, she would say, "We had such a good marriage. It shouldn't have to end like this."

They moved into assisted living, with a pool, a gym, a dining hall, and games and puzzles in the common room. They made friends, as they always did, but they didn't love it. On Ed's ninety-eighth birthday, he blew out the candles on his cake and said, "I wished—for another year!"

"You *did*?" Lou said. "You *want* that? *I* don't want that."

Then a pipe burst in the assisted living building, making the ground floor unusable. That meant no games, no exercise class, all meals delivered to their apartment. The repairs took a long time, and people started getting sick and unhappy.

Ed started waking up earlier and earlier, wanting to roust Lou out of bed as if he were still in the Marines. He put a sticky note on his bathroom mirror to remind him not to. It said, *NO 4 A.M. REVEILLE*. He wanted to make it to one hundred, and he wanted her to want to stay with him.

On her ninety-fifth birthday, I was playing Bananagrams with her, and my cousins kept calling to sing "Happy

Birthday." She told all of them, "*Don't* sing 'And many more!'"
And then she used up all her letters and won.

That year, just after Thanksgiving, she decided she'd had
enough and stopped eating. Her family gathered around her,
taking turns at her bedside. She'd stored up particular memories for each person—things she'd observed or thought about
them, to tell them when they came to hold her hand. When
each of us left her room, we'd go sit with Ed in the living
room. He said, "I know. I know she wants to go." He knew
the force of her will. At night he climbed into bed carefully,
trying not to disturb her.

She slept a lot and kept asking the hospice nurse, "Why is
this taking so long?" But then she would sit up, ask if she could
have a gin and tonic, and tell funny stories all evening. And
sometimes she would be tempted by orange juice. You can live
a surprisingly long time on the occasional gin and tonic and a
little orange juice. It took almost two weeks.

When she died, her two daughters were there to help wash
her body. Her ashes were interred in their local military ceme-
tery. Inner-ear damage from Ed's years as a pilot had made his
balance iffy, so his son rolled him in a wheelchair up the green
hill to the plot. We scattered rose petals and sang "Hey Jude,"
Lou's favorite song. Before we left, Ed leaned forward in the
wheelchair and said to the spot in the ground, "I'll be back."

Ed made it almost to 101, alone now in the lifeboat. He
was still ferociously strong when the physical therapist came to
test him. And he still made jokes. But his memory got shak-
ier. He started confusing his two wars. He missed Lou—his

companion and his great love, but also his prop and his memory aide, the person he tried hardest for, the one he didn't want to let down.

A few weeks before his birthday, he was watching Tiger Woods play golf on TV. His son was sitting with him and watched him nod off and wake up, nod off and wake up. And then Ed didn't wake up. The planned 101st birthday party became a memorial, and Ed went into the ground beside Lou, as he'd promised her he would. No more 4:00 a.m. reveille. Just the lifeboat pulled up on the farthest shore.

The Body Secret

AJA GABEL

The first time I was pregnant, I didn't understand that it was supposed to be a secret and therefore that I, too, was a secret.

After some months of trying, I found out I was pregnant in early March, and I celebrated with my husband in all the ways you're supposed to. We took pictures of the test sticks, cried, fought about eating raw cookie dough, made a list of absurd baby names, and stared at my stomach, willing it to grow. I called a few close friends and told them *six weeks* and was met with hushed tones. *So early*, they said. I told them I wasn't one of those women who was going to keep it a secret from them, because if something bad happened (*something bad*, I always said) I would tell them that part anyway. Isn't it better to have someone with you on the journey than to suffer the bad news alone?

An app gave me size comparisons, and they were as silly as everyone said they'd be. *Your baby is the size of a pea. Your baby is the size of a pumpkin seed.* What the app didn't say: your baby is so small, if you held it, it could slip through your fingers. It didn't say: if you lose a pumpkin seed, don't tell anyone.

When my dad died of stomach cancer at the age of sixty-two, my mother warned me not to tell anyone. She said it would look bad, him dying at that age instead of in his seventies or eighties, as if we had done something wrong or didn't try hard enough. But when you're twenty-one and a senior in college, no one asks why your parent died, or how, or what it looked like. So I stored those details in my head and walked around campus with them, marching toward my future. Only once did they come tumbling out, during my first ever panic attack on a street corner before midterms. Everyone thought I was freaked out about my *Ulysses* exam.

The summer before my dad died, I moved home and spent syrupy warm California afternoons with him. My dad had been a carpenter on construction sites all his life, and I'd never known him not to be doing physical labor. That summer, though, we lazed. We sat on the couch and watched *The Ellen DeGeneres Show*. Sometimes we saw cheap Tuesday matinees. Sometimes I made him smoothies, which he drank only half of while we read books side by side. Sometimes I drove him to chemo, where we cheerfully talked of anything other than the slow poison coursing through his veins.

But those late afternoons on the couch, sometimes I would lie down while he sat, resting my head on his chest and stomach. He had a big Santa Claus belly, though in his post-cancer life it shrank. We watched Ellen dance in the audience, and I listened to the steady beat of his heart. You might think I did this to comfort myself, to hear evidence of his aliveness. But it only scared me. There, beneath my ear was the sound of the fragile mechanism keeping my dad alive—a muscle that at any moment could decide it's had enough. I heard the hush of blood, the creaking of veins adjusting to the work of living. *There it is*, I thought. Not evidence that he was alive but evidence that what was keeping him alive was awfully tender, a mere viscous wish beneath his bones.

I miscarried on a Saturday in April. I'd just eaten pancakes. I rushed from the kitchen to the bathroom and felt, unmistakably, a piece of me that was supposed to be lodged inside my uterus fall with a gentle plop. I stayed in the bathroom awhile, alone, staring at it, memorizing it, before rejoining my husband at the kitchen table and telling him, calmly, "It happened. I think it's over."

I was calm then because the days leading up to it had been the opposite of calm. The cramps were the worst I'd ever felt, flattening me onto the bed, springing tears to my eyes before I could muster up the accompanying sadness, my body knowing before my mind that something was wrong inside. My husband would crouch by the bed and hold my hand, watching my eyes to measure the pain. He did everything he could, but this particular pain wasn't communal. It was deeply private to have my body's shudders teach me about the loss. I couldn't explain it to him while it was happening. I couldn't even explain it to myself. That, too, was part of the grief.

When I was lying there, I thought of the concept of suffering, a childhood fixation of mine. I grew up in the Jodo

Shinshu sect of the Japanese Buddhist Church. Although my mom is Japanese and my dad was white, my dad was the one who dragged us to temple every weekend. And every weekend I learned what suffering meant. According to the Four Noble Truths of Buddhism, we suffer because we're attached to things. I squirmed in my pew and thought of the cartoons I was missing, the pickled daikon I'd be forced to choke down at church lunch after this. I wanted waffles and MTV. I wanted sleeping in and bike riding until dinner. I wanted the things I was attached to. But I sat there and suffered the suffering.

Decades later, I thought of that temple and the teachings as I grasped for anything to get me through the miscarriage cramping. What am I resisting letting go? What could I learn from knowing this suffering is not strange but deeply normal? When the cramps would subside, I would quiet and try to listen. But I heard nothing.

Years after my dad died, I wondered if he, too, thought of those teachings when he was in his final days. One of those days, he was allowed to walk down the hall in his hospital gown and look out the big window at the end, where the sun was setting. I remember him sitting on a chair, staring out that window, wearing an expression that I'd never seen before: anguish. I was upset then because he wasn't looking at me standing next to him, and he wasn't mourning all that he would miss in my life. But now I know he was taking in the world, knowing he wouldn't have it much longer, letting each piece of it go, including me.

A few days later, he told the doctors he wanted to have a final meal. By then, his body had stopped processing food, the tumors on his stomach having spread everywhere, so they sedated him and medically emptied his stomach, preparing him to eat with us one last time. Even now, thinking about this again, I can't tell you what it was like. I can't even tell the other people in the room what it was like. And when it happens to you, you won't be able to tell me. And whoever you're with as they die, they won't be able to tell you. And we will all suffer carrying universal knowledge we can never share.

Miscarriages are incredibly common, and that's part of what made the mourning process painful. How can so many people go through this and so few communicate what it's really like? Are there really legions of women walking around, holding their body's wrenching inside of them? Of course there are. It's the loneliness of having a woman's body, and the loneliness of having a body.

Even more common than having a miscarriage is becoming pregnant, which I did for a second time two months later. This time, I held the secret even closer, which made me feel small as my body grew. Each day I was afraid that the fetus would just slip away, maybe without me even knowing. I watched for signs. I felt terrified at the slightest twitch of pain, and I felt terrified if I felt nothing. My husband told me not to worry, that worrying wouldn't make the baby stay or go, that wasn't how it worked. But he didn't know what it was to be a host to something invisible.

Because I began to worry him with my worry, I kept it to myself more, as I kept the pregnancy in general from my friends and family. It felt lonely there, swirling in that concern, but I learned that it also felt lonely to share it. When I told people about the miscarriage, there were so many wonderful notes from friends, expressing sympathy and love, or confessing that they, too, had gone through it. But even in the notes from the people who'd gone through it and worse, there was no salve or cure. Instead, it was as if the two of us stood in adjacent cells and stared at each other, wondering how to get out. It was nice to have company, but it didn't change the fact that I was locked up.

As I write this, I have yet to tell everyone in my life I'm pregnant. I'm far enough along that I should tell people—I could tell people. But I've felt uneasy about the pregnancy, always worried, confused about what is happening in my body, unsure if I am supposed to celebrate or wait to celebrate: until the baby passes a certain ultrasound scan, until the baby is here, until it's out of the infant stage, until it's walking, until it's talking. But then there's more worry to come: school and friends and happiness, not to mention political disaster, civic disaster, climate disaster. And it's not just worry about the baby's life that keeps me swallowing the news of my pregnancy. It's worry about myself, too. Am I doing it right now, and will I do it right later? I'm upset I can't eat what I want, go where I want, and wear what I want. Sometimes I break into sobs at episodes of *The West Wing* or *The Great British Baking Show*. Sometimes I look at my body and feel sad I might never again look like I used to look. There's so much to do wrong, and yet I continue to swell.

The thing no one told me about pregnancy is that when you are pregnant, you carry a secret, and so you are a secret to yourself. You are also a secret to your partner. You carry this alone. You cannot truly share the pain of growing life, just as you cannot truly share the pain of letting life go.

For hours after doctors declared my father formally deceased, my family and I stayed in the hospice room with him, with his body. We didn't discuss leaving, but we also didn't discuss staying. The staff came and went, asking us if we needed anything, but they never told us what to do, one way or another. My mother called the reverend of our temple, and we waited.

I remember sitting on the corner of the bed his body lay on, and thinking, *This is just his body. He is no longer here. I no longer feel him here.* I never believed in spirits or souls before that, and I'm not sure I believe in them now in exactly the way some people do, but that day I gathered together not a belief but an assurance (is that what faith feels like?) that a person and a body are separate things, distinct clusters of energy that do what they want, sometimes in opposing directions. That's what cancer was inside my dad, growing and regrowing and jumping from organ to organ despite everything he did to stop it. And that's what my dad was, despite the cancer, a man who enjoyed cooking, liked to look at the stars and planets, and cared for the family's small dog in the lonely days of his final years. Each a distinct entity: the person and the body.

The reason I know this is because, as the feeling of my father receded with the terrible knowledge that he would never open his eyes again, his body swelled. When the reverend showed up after we'd been sitting there for hours, I saw her see it too. He was huge. He was a decomposing body; he was not my father anymore. Yet as his body expanded, I thought of those afternoons I spent with him the summer before, lying with my head on his chest, trying to get as close to his thumping heart as possible, even though it scared me. I knew that I had been right: our bodies are our most-kept secrets.

Round ligament pain is a sharp jabbing pain during pregnancy that happens in your lower abdomen as your uterus grows and stretches to accommodate the baby. Some nights I'm awoken by it, a feeling I at first confuse for having to pee, then confuse for a contraction; then I settle into the understanding that it's the wrenching of my body expanding. Sometimes I joke about poking my husband's stomach with something sharp so he'll understand what it feels like, but even then, I know he wouldn't really know. The pain has to come from the inside.

Last night as I was roused by the sharp jabbing, I thought about this. I looked at my husband, sleeping soundly next to me. I know there's more expansion and more pain to come later in the pregnancy and labor, the sort I can't even imagine right now. And I won't really be able to share the suffering with him, no matter how hard I squeeze his hand or scream or bleed.

My husband's father is also gone. He died a couple of months before our first date. On that date, I asked him about it. He was taken aback at first, and told me people don't usually bring it up. I told him that when my dad died, people also didn't ask me about it, for fear of upsetting me, but I was upset anyway, all day, every day. And when people didn't even try to ask, I felt even more alone in that pain. So I make a point to ask people how they're doing if they've newly lost someone.

Recently, my husband told me that moment on our first date was part of what made him fall in love with me, that I opened myself so clearly to him right away, to a part of him that might be painful and ugly. I was surprised when he said that, knowing that I could never carry his grief, the way he can never carry mine. But I came to understand that it didn't matter. It only mattered that I'd asked, that I'd offered to stand in the same prison with him, at least for a little while. The company was nice, because the loneliness of grief was a hard burden to bear.

In bed next to my husband, I tried to remember if the reverend had said any wise words when she came to the hospice where my father lay. In my memory, she said nothing, only laid her hand on his shoulder and remained there with us. Maybe she did that because there was nothing to say. Yes, life is suffering and suffering is attachment and we are attached to our fathers and mothers and partners and children, and also our pets who can't speak and the planets we've never been to and sometimes unborn fetuses. And eventually, all of us have to loosen the grip of our attachment and let go. Everyone is a secret made of mysterious enzymes and hormones, anger and desires. I don't know this baby expanding my body, though I am literally attached to it, one secret body making another. What matters is that we *try*: to cross the distance from me to you, from my strange body to yours, from my loneliness to yours. This pain in my abdomen—it's the crossing.

The Perpetual Foreigner

JEAN KWOK

Every day, my parents and brothers disappeared to work in a clothing factory in New York's Chinatown. After school, my father picked me up and took me there too. Even though I was still just in kindergarten when I started, I worked, because for us, every cent counted. During our breaks, the other children working there played tag between enormous racks of clothing. Because I was such a recent immigrant and didn't live in Chinatown like the other kids, I was tolerated but never befriended. When the inspectors came, though, we all hid together, lying buried under mounds of clothing in the huge bins, taking shallow breaths, trying not to be heard even as we struggled not to suffocate.

When I was a child in Hong Kong, I wasn't lonely. I was without consciousness, fearless in my home environment, not realizing that anything could ever change. I sat on the back of my brother's bicycle and hollered for him to go faster until we crashed into a fruit stand, spilling mangos and lychee nuts everywhere. I sipped red bean ice in the teahouse, swinging my legs, while my father drank oolong tea and smoked with his business cronies. I'd never been told that my formerly wealthy family had been trying to escape from Communist China to the United States for years or that Hong Kong, where I was born, was one of the stops on their long journey. One day when I was five years old, we left in a taxi for the airport. I kept looking through the rear window, watching my home shrink until it disappeared altogether. I didn't know then that for many years, I would cling to these memories, that small golden patch of sunlight in my life.

The move to America cost us everything: The monetary toll of lost income, plane tickets, years of lawyers' fees, visas, paperwork. But the heavier price was losing our language, our friends, our culture, and in some ways, one another. We were placed by a relative in an apartment in the slums of Brooklyn that didn't have a working central heating system. It was over-run with roaches and rats. The windows in the back had been shattered, and throughout the bitter New York winters, the wind would gust against the garbage bags we used to cover up the holes. We kept the oven on, with the door open, day and night to generate a small circle of warmth, but still, the remaining panes of glass were covered with a thick layer of ice on the inside that I would try to melt with my bluing fingers.

Our poverty didn't hurt me in the expected ways. I didn't see the shabby walls or the holes in our drapes, and although I did long for an American Barbie, believing that the pos-session of one would make me tall and blond as well, I was an imaginative child who got lost in dreams as easily as toys. What did wound me were the scornful looks the other girls at school gave my homemade clothing, the red marks all over my spelling tests, the way the teacher blushed when I asked to borrow a rubber (British English for an eraser), the sweat-filled exhaustion that overcame my brothers and left them unable to play with me, the skin underneath my nose that cracked and bled due to my constant colds in our freezing apartment. I had left so much back in Hong Kong: my prowess in school, my sparkly gold slippers, my much-admired ability to curse as well as the fishmonger, my afternoons wandering the sunlit streets with my brothers and my fat ginger cat.

Perhaps a greater burden than the poverty itself was the need to keep our circumstances a secret. How can you ease your loneliness when no one knows who you truly are? I did try to tell the truth once. When a classmate asked why I was never home when she called me, I told her it was because I worked in a factory after school. The next day, she informed me that she had asked her father, a Yale-educated lawyer, and he'd told her that I was lying because children didn't work in factories in America. I learned to keep my mouth shut.

I filled the void of my loneliness with another emotion: ambition. I burned to leave the life we were trapped in. I didn't dream of being rich; I dreamed of being great. I wanted to be brilliant, worthy of admiration; I wanted to shake this world, where my tongue still tripped over the foreign words.

However, I knew better than to speak of such things in my traditional Chinese home, where I was not only the youngest of seven children but a girl at that. The family social hierarchy was determined by age and gender, and by both standards, I was at rock bottom. I was supposed to be as pliant as the tender dumplings they expected me to make, yet I had no interest in cleaning, cooking, or growing up to become a patient, supportive wife. My family threw up their hands. I was so stubborn and clumsy, always with my nose buried in a library book, never responding to help sweep the floor when called. How would they ever find a man willing to marry me?

From a young age, I understood the trajectory of the road ahead of me. I would work at the clothing factory, progressing upward to the better-paying jobs, and peaking when I became one of the young women who worked on the sewing machines, racing from garment to garment, the needles piercing the vulnerable cloth. After that would come the decline, until I ended up as one of the old ladies who cut the loose threads off of buttonholes, hobbling home with extra garments, the plastic handles cutting into my calloused palms. The only alternative route—and the one I understood comprised my family's unspoken dream—was for me to escape this life by finding a nice young man to marry. Then I could cook and clean for him, support him while he finished his education, bear him sons, and take care of them while he worked.

I decided I would go to Harvard instead. It was the one college my immigrant family had heard of; it was the one school they couldn't refuse. If I wasn't accepted there, I might not be allowed to go to college at all.

Thus my process of self-education began. I memorized every word in my ragged dictionary. After reading every book in the children's section of the public library, I moved on to the adult ones. The other kids didn't know what to make of me. My mother made my clothing. My brothers cut my hair. Neither of these things added to my coolness. Although I spoke English by then, I didn't understand cooties or cryptic phrases that somehow meant your fly was open.

When I was eleven, I tested into Hunter College High School, a public school for the intellectually gifted. There, I met kids brighter than any I had ever encountered before. I was both comforted and awed. On the one hand, I no longer had to worry about being called the "Queen of the Brains," as one girl had written in my elementary school autograph book. On the other, I felt outclassed. When I had chosen a foreign language the summer before school started, I had picked Latin at random, not realizing until the first day of class that it was a dead language. A handful of kids were already fluent in French, a language I inferred was cultured and beautiful, unlike my native Chinese. I was learning to place Europeans on a pedestal, above humble immigrants of color like myself. It wouldn't be until years later that I thought to question this implicit hierarchy. While sharing our favorite books, I told a boy that mine was *Anne of Green Gables*. His was Immanuel Kant's *Critique of Pure Reason*. On the bus, a group of kids in the back formed a mini-Senate and their shouts of "Filibuster,

filibuster, filibuster!" formed the backdrop to my rides back to my own home, where there were no books except for the ones I'd received for free from the public library's literacy programs.

Needless to say, I didn't tell anyone about my background. When a social studies teacher I greatly admired decided to give us daily current events quizzes, I failed them every day. Not only were there no English newspapers at home, but I had no context to understand any of those events and no one to explain them to me. When the teacher asked me why I was flunking, I lied. When I was invited to parties or movies, I lied. I couldn't tell my friends that I wasn't allowed. My family didn't want me to do anything but attend school. I wasn't even permitted to accept a job at a molecular biology laboratory at Sloan-Kettering in my senior year of high school, but I did anyway. When my brother asked me where I went after school, I lied. I had carved myself into slices like a melon and there was no one who saw the entirety of who I was.

When I was accepted early to Harvard, I couldn't wait to embrace my independence. Intellectually, I blossomed in college. Socially, I met kids who jetted off to weekends in the Bahamas. At certain private parties, they would swipe all the dishes off the tables at the end of the meal to prove how uninhibited and decadent they were, leaving the mess of food and broken crockery for scholarship students like me to clean up. I didn't feel the urge to tell anyone about how my mother used to fall asleep over bags of unfinished clothing from the factory every night.

At the social service organization at Harvard where I

worked with Asian American immigrants, I met other students who may have had backgrounds similar to mine, but
I still kept silent. As I became an adult, I slowly realized that
after years of hiding who I truly was, I was no longer able to
reveal myself.

Then I met a Dutch man while I was backpacking through
Honduras the summer before I would start my MFA in fiction
at Columbia. Standing on the hot beach in my Birkenstocks, I
idly swatted at sand flies with one hand while the other shaded
my eyes from the glare of the sun against the azure water. The
air smelled of rich spices. I was behind the Dutch guy on line
for dinner, where someone scooped a heaping helping of pork,
sweet plantains, pickled onions, beans, and rice from a giant
pot onto our plates for a dollar each.

When he turned to me, I braced myself for yet another
slick come-on line. "Did you know that your teeth are too
big for your mouth?" he said. Surprised, I laughed. This was
true. My orthodontist had told me the same thing but no one
had ever noticed before, especially since the problem had been
fixed. Yes, this was a slightly critical comment from a near
stranger, but it disarmed me. I'd just quit my job as a professional ballroom dancer, which I'd taken after college as a day
job so I could write. I'd been asked out a lot in those years,
almost always by men who would smoothly move on to the
next dancer when I said no. We were interchangeable to them.
It was a breath of fresh air to be seen.

The Dutch man turned out to be equally perceptive in
emotional areas, and we fell in love. I hadn't understood how

heavy the burden of loneliness had been upon me until it was lightened. I felt tremendous relief to have found someone who knew whether I was happy or sad, no matter which mask I might have adopted.

On our honeymoon, I braved returning to Hong Kong. I had long resisted because I had always been aware in the deepest part of me that my fantasy of home, of a place where I truly belonged, would be eradicated by the new me, the one who grew up in Brooklyn instead of Kowloon. And indeed it was so. I loved being back—the warm pineapple buns, bowing to the Kuan Yin at temples—but everyone knew I was a foreigner, including me. It was in the way I walked, my clothing, my makeup, my accent, the white husband following me around.

It wasn't until we moved to the Netherlands and I became an immigrant for the second time that I realized how much of our identities are reflected back upon us by other people. When you tell someone you went to a particular university, he or she recognizes it and is impressed or not. When you mention the town you lived in, your conversational partner says, "Oh, I know someone from there." These echoes reaffirm who we think we are, for good or for bad. In the Netherlands, though, I cast my facts into the void. No one knew Park Slope or Cantonese or hamantaschen or thousand-year-old eggs. The Dutch language was incomprehensible to me. Screwing up my nerve, I would go to the store, reciting the phrase I had learned in Dutch class, "Where is the shampoo? Where is the shampoo?" When I dared attempt this with the clerk, she would respond with a flood of unfathomable words that chased me out the door as I fled.

I do speak Dutch now and we have two children. Whereas I used to come home feeling slightly wounded by Dutch honesty every day, I have learned to value such directness. The Netherlands is a wonderful place to live, with excellent health care, schooling, and a very relaxed attitude toward raising kids. However, I still always find myself just a bit out of sync with everyone else. The Dutch are the tallest people in the world, and I am barely five feet tall. When I pick the kids up from school, I am lost in a forest of tree trunks. Voices float far above my head. I need to jump up and down in public bathrooms to catch a glimpse of my face. When all of the other Dutch moms agree that it's perfectly all right for a bunch of eleven-year-olds to camp by themselves on the public beach, I'm the one who says, "Isn't that the infamous spot for hookups?" As soon as the canal by our house is covered by the thinnest layer of ice in the winter, all of our neighbors fearlessly rush out and skate on it. Those who cannot skate, stand. Why? I do not know. Never having felt truly American, I realize how American I have become.

As someone who has been an immigrant twice, I have spent most of my life feeling lonely. In fact, I still do. I often feel slightly out of step with everyone else around me, translating different versions of myself back and forth.

This is a part of the price of being a foreigner. We are

pulled by language, culture, the enormous mass of our invisible pasts that both weigh us down and give us our gravitas. Sometimes I think back to my time in the factory as a child, hiding from the inspectors under a mountain of clothing in those enormous bins, struggling to breathe. Yet even then, I had a quiet determination not only to keep breathing but one day to rise, fling all of that fabric aside, and finally allow myself to be seen.

The Woman Who Walked Alone

AMY SHEARN

Once upon a time in New York City, a thirty-year-old Eastern European immigrant named Lillian Alling decided, like
so many before her and so many since, to say "goodbye to
all that." For unconfirmed reasons—though there have been
many guesses, including that she was trying to reunite with a
lover, or with a child, or that she just really hated the city—
Lillian struck out from New York City to Siberia. On foot.
Allegedly she was trying to reconnect with her people, exiled
Eastern European Jews who had gone to settle the promised
land of Siberia. The walk took her three years, but she made it,
or almost made it, or spectacularly did not make it, depending
whom you ask.

Lillian worked as a domestic or perhaps in the garment industry; she was poor, single, and would never be able to save up
the passage for a steamer back home, even in steerage. Instead

she took a bag full of bread and tea, and some maps she'd hand-copied from the New York Public Library, and crossed from New York State into Canada. It was Christmas Eve 1926, a brisk time for taking an extended stroll.

Canada kept scant records of European immigrants at the time, so there is not much of a paper trail. Lillian never published anything about her journey or motivations and she resisted people's efforts to interview or photograph her. But every-where she went, she piqued people's curiosity, and by the time she reached Canada, newspaper and magazine articles were being written about the mysterious walking woman.

Somehow she made it across the country all the way to the West Coast, perhaps by tracing the railroad tracks or occasion-ally hitching a ride on the train itself. She trekked up moun-tains and across terrains that challenged the most seasoned of hikers, and she did it wearing only a dress, ordinary tennis shoes, and a head cloth to protect herself from insects.

She always walked alone.

I am listening to a podcast about Lillian with my face stuffed into someone's armpit on a sardine-packed subway train at rush hour, heading home after work, anxious about picking up my kids on time, and all I can think about is how great her quest sounds. The idea of taking off into the unknown burdened with fewer supplies than I currently carry in my everyday tote bag seems like a dream. I long to be somewhere still, with land and sky. Even being cold and underfed—because I am at that moment overwarm and overfull and sweat is trickling down my back—sounds bracing and life-affirming. And the idea of being alone and clearheaded, of missing people instead of feeling crowded out of my own brain by them, of experiencing the connective state of solitude rather than the alienation I feel in this exaggerated, 1980s-movie-style commuter crowd of strangers, sounds as refreshing as a dip in a Yukon creek.

I am a married, working mother of two school-age children and I am in a backward state; I feel lonely, sometimes desperately so, and yet I am never alone. It doesn't make sense, which bothers me. Because what am I lonely for? Whom am I missing? How can I feel lonely when I am never alone?

Lonely implies a lack; *lonely* involves missing someone. It used to be that when I picked up my then-tiny daughter from her morning playgroup, she would say, "I was so lonely for you!" In her intuitive little-kid way she'd pinpointed something about loneliness. Being *alone* implies a place, a solid state, but being *lonely* is a condition, directional, an exchange or, rather, a missed exchange.

Maybe I feel lonely *because* I am never alone.

Around this same time I feel a strange compulsion to reread my journal from the moment in my life when, it now seems to me, I was living most authentically, when I was seeking adventure, fearlessly independent—notebooks I had never re-read until now, nearly twenty years after writing them—my journal from when I spent the summer backpacking alone around Europe. *How can I ever be that girl again?* I now think self-pityingly—remembering my solitary strolls through Paris, Barcelona, Venice, remembering how I cultivated aimless-ness, turning down one street because it smelled nice, head-ing up another because I liked the way its buildings reflected the sun, following only my own inner compass—as I steal a twenty-minute walk to do errands during my lunch break, the only inkling of a journey I'll be able to take in the fore-seeable future. *How can I be as purely* me *as when I was always alone?* my brain moans to itself as I load the dishwasher in the careless way my husband hates, because I cannot summon the energy within to give the household chores any more of myself than they already get, while he watches television in the other room. *How can I*—even just the thought is interrupted, inevi-tably, with a "MAAAMMMMAAA?"

I shepherd my children through dinner, homework, bath time, bedtime. Once they're asleep, I read my travel journal, over several nights, in bed, like a thriller.

Like Lillian, I am in my thirties and of indistinct Eastern Euro-pean Jewish heritage; like Lillian, I lack any skills of particular interest to the current economy. Like Lillian, I find that my ordinary life dissatisfies me. Some days the restlessness feels like an actual physical condition, roiling in my gut.

Unlike Lillian, however, I am a wife and mother, facts that anchor me firmly to the ground. I live in a big apartment building in New York City, and I work on an editorial staff, and I am a semi-engaged community member. My brain teems with input and responsibilities and various competing roles. I crave time to myself, but I am always among people, every moment of every day: at work, at home with my children, in bed with my spouse. I appreciate my city for its often interesting crowds, and my workplace for its quiet hours of companionable keyboard-clacking, but my default mode is not seeking out the company of others—at heart I've always been more of a low-rent Greta Garbo, moaning, "I want to be alone!"

In her book *The Lonely City*, Olivia Laing writes about artists who inhabit crowded cities in lonely ways, "hyper-alert to the gulfs between people, to how it can feel to be islanded amid the crowd." My guess is that's what happened to Lillian. New York City was both too crowded and too lonely a place for her—she told people along the way that she had been unable to make either money or friends there. Islanded amid the crowd. To Lillian, solitude, her long walk alone—especially if she was in fact headed home, or to a person who felt like home—must have seemed like the least lonely option.

Lillian's story feeds my wanderlust at a time when my life does not. The routine—subway, gym, office, subway, home, repeat—feels like it's slowly compressing me into a dulled nub of the person I used to be, or was meant to be.

It takes me a long time—years, actually—to understand that I am unhappy, and that I am unhappy for a specific reason, and that this reason is both simple and complicated: my marriage. It's a lonely marriage. He works long hours, he stays out late, he spends a lot of the weekend sleeping. Even when we do spend time together, we can't seem to connect. Our disconnected state becomes blaringly obvious when the kids are in bed and we are alone in a room together and I say, "Hey, you're so quiet, what's on your mind?" and without looking up from his phone or the television he'll say, "Nothing," and then "But if you want to talk, go ahead and talk."

And sometimes I do, I just sort of talk toward him, because I am hungry for human connection, because I long for conversation, because I have something to process or share or a neat thing I noticed that day that I want to show-and-tell to someone, and I'll talk, and it will feel like nothing so much as being a little kid and getting chatty at bedtime, hoping that if you can be charming enough you'll distract your mom from turning out the light and leaving the room. I dangle questions and try out conversation starters I've gathered from things I've read about keeping the flame alive and all that. I chat, I twirl, I try to dazzle. He nods, sometimes, when I've paused and he can tell it's time to nod. The only measurable way it feels different from talking to myself is that sometimes he runs out of patience and says, "Is this really a story or just another random observation?"

We are inert bodies that happen to share the same space. But that's what marriage is, after a while, right? "Well, good-night then," I'll eventually say and go finish up any household chores that need to get accomplished, and then go to bed, alone.

To occupy my brain, I consume every bit of information I can find about Lillian, including nonfiction accounts, a novel, a graphic novel, and a poetic short film. There's an opera about her too—I listen to snippets on YouTube while the children wonder why dinner's taking so long.

Her trip up the West Coast is much better documented than the initial cross-country leg of her travels, because she walked up the Telegraph Trail, a rough footpath along the lines bringing telegraph access from southern Canada up to Dawson City in the Yukon Territory. What she didn't know was that the telegraph line had never actually been completed. By the time of Lillian's walk along the hypothetical telegraph, there were five open stations, one every fifty miles of what had been built of the trail, each manned by a lineman whose responsibility it was to keep his section of the telegraph line in good repair. The trail existed in order to facilitate conversation, to join countries together, like an international tin-can-and-string phone. It strikes me as a rather bald metaphor, foreshadowing the information age: here is Lillian, walking alone, along a leap of imagination designed to connect people.

Yet Lillian was decidedly not walking in order to connect with people. By some accounts, all she would say when the station linemen talked to her or tried to offer assistance was "I go to Siberia." She traveled holding a lead pipe as a weapon, so perhaps at this point she'd had experience being offered the kind of assistance she did not desire.

On September 19, 1927, when she showed up at the first cabin, the operator worried she wouldn't make it on foot so late in the season. Presumably he tried to talk her out of continuing before what he did next, which was to call the local constable and have her arrested. The men decided to keep her in jail for the winter, charging her with vagrancy, in order, they said, to save her life. And why not? Men have long locked up women in prisons of various sorts, with the excuse of protecting them from their own wild ideas.

When I excitedly tell people about Lillian Alling and her long walk, they often squint at me and ask whether she was mentally ill. When this happens I don't include the part about how I think her quest sounds delightful and tempting to imitate. Then again, I'm uniquely primed to love her story, as it falls into a genre I'm fascinated by that I guess could be essentially summed up as Women Running Away from Their Lives. I love the novels *Where'd You Go, Bernadette?*, *Nine Months*, and *Norma Jean the Termite Queen*; I obsess over the 1970 movie *Wanda* (and the Wanda-adjacent book *Suite for Barbara Loden*). I delight in the story of Emma Gatewood, a sixty-seven-year-old woman who one day in 1955 told her family she needed some fresh air and was going out for a walk and ended up hiking the entire Appalachian Trail. Who among us has never needed that much fresh air? I know I shouldn't relate to these woman so hard; I have a totally fine and socially acceptable life, and of course in actuality I would never walk away from my children.

And yet.

What bothers people about Lillian, I think, is that they can't understand exactly *what* her difficult quest was. Her motives were uncomfortably vague, perhaps even to herself, and she never seemed inclined to explain herself. I think this is also exactly what I love about her. I admire anyone who has the conviction to do a wild thing, even if they can't fully explain it in a way people will understand.

After Lillian's six months in jail she worked for a while in Vancouver and then took off again up the Telegraph Trail. There is a photograph of her with a dog that according to most accounts was given to her by one of the linemen. The dog, her only walking companion on her entire trip, soon died—probably from eating poison bait left out for wolverines—and there is at least one story, unsubstantiated but oddly appealing, that she stuffed the dog and traveled with the DIY-taxidermized pet for some time.

Having walked up the Telegraph Trail, with or perhaps without a jaunty stuffed dog corpse, resisting the linemen's attempts to better outfit her for the weather or to convince her to give up her quest, Lillian found domestic work in Dawson City. There locals described her as being "ignorant" and "uncouth." Imagine this independent, wild woman, pent up working, after all those months of walking and sleeping outside and fending for herself! I'm sure she was uncouth! As the reality show saw goes, she was not there to make friends.

In 1929, an anthropologist on an expedition for the Smithsonian reported seeing a mysterious white woman traveling the Yukon River in an odd-looking boat. He wrote: "Everybody speculates about her strange proceedings, but those who spoke to her say she is not insane. 'Writes novels,' or 'perhaps a criminal.'"

●

How far did she get? A fellow Lillian obsessive, the whimsical world traveler Lawrence Millman, writes in his 2012 *Hiking to Siberia*:

> For my book, I decided to follow in Lillian's footsteps wherever possible, so I set out to hike at least a portion of the Yukon Telegraph Trail myself. Unfortunately, it was no longer a trail by this time, and I soon found myself plodding through a boreal hell composed of muskeg, virtually impenetrable undergrowth, and devil's club, a plant armed with cat-claw spines. I was under constant assault by horse flies and mosquitos, which seemed to work in tandem with each other. Here and there I saw skeins of old telegraph wire, and at one point I encountered a moose skeleton wrapped in wire like a mummy . . . After five very unpleasant days, I gave up. But Lillian did not give up.

No, Lillian did not give up. She was reported to have left Nome, on Alaska's coast, by boat, in 1929. Natives frequently traveled between Siberia and Alaska via the Bering Strait. Perhaps someone was able to help Lillian travel across the water in a traditional watercraft. Some sources reported that she tried to swim across the Bering Strait and drowned. Others swear they saw her cross the strait by boat.

•

At this very moment, I'm so crowded and restless in my daily life that I feel I am an instant away from screaming at the top of my lungs. But what can I do? I treat my feelings like a junkie feeding an old addiction with a synthetic version of the favored drug: *Here, Wanderlust, have a walk in the park. Okay, Independence, you can have an hour to yourself, fine, but not too often.* I want to work on my latest novel but that doesn't pay the bills, so I go to my stultifying job and then I come home and pick up the kids. I put another frozen pizza in the pizza-cheese-encrusted oven. I load the dishwasher. I help the kids with homework and tell them they have to get off their screens and take baths and read books with actual words and all the other annoying things mothers have to do. When my husband gets home I ask him about his day, and he grunts a response, doesn't ask about mine, goes into the other room. I think about Lillian.

Sometimes it's Lillian's solitude that I envy. But it's more than just that; it's her wildness and her singularity of purpose. She wanted one thing: to walk, alone, in the direction of home. Isn't that what all of us want, really? Isn't that what life is, actually? In Amy Bloom's novelization of Lillian's life, *Away*, the fictionalized Lillian learns that the daughter she thought was killed in a pogrom back home is indeed alive, and her desire to find her child lends her a tangible backstory, an understandable motive. But in real life I wonder if Lillian's goal was even less rational, even more primal: just to *go*.

We don't tend to like wildness or independence in women, particularly in women over the age of thirty, which Laing describes as the "age at which female aloneness . . . carries with it a persistent whiff of strangeness, deviance and failure." We like wildness even less in mothers. Kim Brooks writes in her essay "Portrait of the Artist as a Young Mom" that "the point of art is to unsettle, to question, to disturb what is comfortable and safe. And that shouldn't be anyone's goal as a parent." Rufi Thorpe writes in her essay "Mother, Writer, Monster, Maid" that "there is no surer way to locate your self, if you have misplaced her for a moment, than to ask yourself what you want . . . And there is nothing more subversive for a woman to do than believe she deserves to get what she wants and to recognize in herself the willingness to fight to get it."

I try to conjure the version of myself who would take on an impossible quest, who would fight for what she wants, even if it's subversive or socially unacceptable or hard to explain to the world. And then I actually do it.

•

I leave my husband and move out, into my own place.

It has taken me years to admit to myself that my restlessness and loneliness aren't just part of who I am. In fact all along they were symptoms of a fatally ill marriage, despite how I tied myself in knots trying to make them be about something else, a personal flaw perhaps or just an inevitable characteristic of modern middle-aged life.

I strike out alone because my married life is too lonely. I actually do it.

Now, I'm alone for some of each week, when my children are at their dad's a couple of blocks away. Something in me unfurls. I write, and I think. I listen to the music I like and no one makes fun of it; I read old favorite books that curl up in my brain like cats. I talk to friends on the phone for longer than I've been able to in years. I can connect with people in ways that were frowned upon in the subculture of my marriage: I spontaneously have friends over for mugs of wine in my almost-unpacked apartment; when my kids have playdates, I can invite their friends to stay for dinner; we are invited to share meals with other families and I don't have to make an excuse, and I can say yes and find myself having interesting conversations with neighbors and acquaintances I'd only vaguely known before. Maybe I'll date someday, I think. Maybe someday I'll fall in love, although that concept sounds, right now, to me, like science fiction.

I feel like myself for the first time in ages. I have energy and attention to spare. When my children are with me, I parent them the way I want to—with focus and patience and generosity and curiosity. As Anne Morrow Lindbergh writes in *Gift from the Sea*, "If one is out of touch with oneself, then one cannot touch others . . . Only when one is connected to one's own core is one connected to others." And that core, she notes, is so often found in solitude.

The restlessness has quelled. The unhappiness evaporated.

My ex-husband doesn't understand what has happened, being under the impression that in the absence of physical abuse or infidelity there can be no sane reason to leave a marriage. I can't get him to understand, but I can remind myself that no matter how it may look on the outside, I am in fact a reasonable human being on a very difficult quest. My inner Lillian reminds me not to worry about controlling the narrative. She never bothered to correct people who made up their own stories about her. She knew that the only story that matters is the one you're living, no matter how many men ask you to explain yourself in their terms.

I plan long walks. Maybe this weekend I'll walk all the way to the ocean. Maybe someday I'll travel farther, but at the moment I feel content. I no longer feel like I'm wearing one of those lead vests they give you for X-rays at the dentist's office. I have my children and my work and my friends and my family and I have time to just be myself, and I feel extremely, ecstatically unlonely.

When I start to lose my nerve, I remember Lillian, walking toward "home," whatever that may be. Maybe I'm walking that path right now.

Part and Apart

PETER HO DAVIES

Coventry, England, is a nondescript place, not famous for much—Lady Godiva rode naked through its streets to protest taxes, according to medieval legend, and the Luftwaffe bombed it flat one night in 1940—so it's understandable the city would want to claim Philip Larkin, probably the finest, if dourest, British postwar poet. A plaque at the railway station quotes his lines about passing through the town by train: "'Why, Coventry!' I exclaimed. 'I was born here.'"

So, as it happens, was I (though, mixed race as I am, I didn't always look it). I even went to the same school as Larkin, albeit fifty years later; my first ever publication as a spotty teenager was in a copy of the school magazine that also featured an interview with him.

What the plaque omits are Larkin's less flattering memories of the city "where my childhood was unspent" and especially the same poem's final damning line, "Nothing, like something, happens anywhere," which when I first read it in school enraged and dismayed me in equal measure, not because it wasn't true, but because it was *still* true all those years on from Larkin's youth. Even those few famous happenings of the past seemed oddly like nothing—the bombing that reduced the city center to nothing, Godiva's wearing nothing (even her nakedness was a nonevent, unobserved by the townsfolk who stayed indoors out of respect, all but the tailor, Peeping Tom, blinded for his impiety). As for the present, or at least the early 1980s of my youth, the lyrics of a more recent poet, Jerry Dammers, another alum of my school and now leader of the Specials, summed it up perfectly: "This town is coming like a ghost town."

"Ghost Town" was the anthem of a troubled summer. Coventry wasn't the only dying town in Margaret Thatcher's Britain. Violent unrest—a result of rising unemployment and racial tensions—broke out in inner cities across the country in London, Birmingham, Liverpool, and Manchester. We waited, braced for trouble in Coventry. And while I was relieved when it didn't flare up . . . there it was again, that creeping sense of living in a place where nothing ever happened.

But then at the end of that summer of "Ghost Town," *something*—in the eyes of a nerdy child, at least—did happen in Coventry: a *Star Trek* convention came to town. (And if this leap from Philip Larkin via Jerry Dammers to James Kirk makes you do a double take, that's just a hint of how unlikely the prospect of a *Star Trek* convention in Coventry was to me at the time.) This was 1981. Conventions had been attracting crowds of fans in the United States for a decade and were partly credited with the revival of the show in movie form. I had *read* about them in fanzines and movie magazines and they seemed like legendary gatherings of mythical beings up there with Camelot and the Fellowship of the Ring. Frankly, the idea of one beaming down in Coventry seemed about as likely as the *Enterprise* itself appearing in the skies above our church spires. And to make the whole thing more improbably magical, the convention was due in town . . . on my fourteenth birthday. Clearly, not only did I have to see it to believe it, but I was destined to attend.

Science fiction—not the more literary figures like Larkin or George Eliot, who I learned years later based her fictional Middlemarch on Coventry—was what first made me want to write. It was what I first loved to read and watch and, thanks to fan magazines, behind-the-scenes making-of documentaries, and a book called *Who Writes Science Fiction?** (a series of *Paris Review*–style interviews conducted by Charles Platt with science fiction luminaries from Golden Age lions like Asimov and Bradbury to new-wave bad boys like Harlan Ellison and Michael Moorcock), the first fiction that I could imagine creating. But writing it—lousy knockoff space opera, written not coincidentally in front of our TV—was itself only a means to an end, an entry to a community that seemed both improbably cool and warmly welcoming . . . if only it weren't, for the most part, on the other side of the Atlantic.

---

* Published as *Dream Makers* in the United States.

There's a telling image in my head, even now, forty years later, something I never even saw a photo of, just read about: Harlan Ellison, also the author of the iconic *Star Trek* episode "The City on the Edge of Forever," at some convention sitting in a plastic pyramid writing a story while hundreds watch him work. It's a bravura stunt—one he also performed in various bookstore windows—that still strikes me, as it did in my youth, as *awesome*. But the passage of years also makes it seem like something more, an emblem of some writerly desire to be at once alone and even aloof and yet also at the center of the crowd. To be part and apart simultaneously. To be the most important part, at that. And though I couldn't have expressed it at the time, that's what I was yearning for in my first convention. That's all.

Of course, it was awful. There was not another kid to be seen, and my shy teenage self was mortified by all these *adults* sharing my passion (all with resolutely drab British names: Viv and Terry, Mick and Sue, Tim and Cilla). Confronted by my future—it was a sci-fi convention after all—I suddenly realized that I secretly shared my parents' hope that fandom was just a passing phase. The middle-aged ladies in Starfleet minidresses especially appalled me (they weren't quite as naked as Godiva, but I averted my eyes anyway). But I was also not above some self-mortification. At one ignominious low point I bought myself a *Star Trek* birthday card and stood patiently in line to have George Takei, Nichelle Nichols, Grace Lee Whitney, and Mark Lenard sign it for me (all so graciously that none of them betrayed a flicker of pity).

And then there was the filk (science fiction folk music), acoustic numbers about tribbles and warp speed, which in Jerry Dammers's ghost town felt if not quite sacrilegious, certainly apocalyptically uncool.

It feels like a desperate, even reckless, act of loneliness in retrospect—though maybe all fandom, with its inevitably one-way sense of connection, is lonely—but back then my worst moment of the convention was something seemingly much more innocuous. Some gala event was starting in the hotel ballroom—the costume competition, maybe—and painfully self-conscious of sitting alone, I thought I'd find a perch on a staircase, high enough for a good view but hidden away at the rear of the room. A part and apart. A few people had already gathered there—it seemed a quietly companionable spot—but almost as soon as I found a place at the rail someone asked to see my convention badge. The staircase, it turned out, was reserved for organizers, lighting crew, and photographers. Of course it was. No one was especially mean about it (merely British) but I fled anyway—not quite in tears, not quite running, but taking the steps two at a time, not even looking for another seat.

It's the loneliest I've ever felt (which probably makes me lucky), but why? I've been in cities of millions where I didn't speak the language. I've been hiking on mountainsides where I couldn't see another soul for miles.

All this, I should stress, was before the recent mainstreaming of nerd culture, when fandom still had a taint of the furtive, the aberrant even (fan fiction's preoccupation with the sex and sexuality of beloved characters still felt transgressive, because most sex and sexuality back then, especially in Britain, *was* transgressive). I went to the convention *alone* because I was too ashamed to tell anyone else I was going. I went feeling lonely already, with the hope of finding my people there. Seeking out new life and new civilizations. And they were my people in many ways—they read and watched and loved many of the things I read and watched and loved—and yet, even there among this gathering of nerds and weirdos, I still felt like an outsider. How weird did that make me? It's the worst loneliness, I think, the loneliness we feel among those we feel we should be most like, most want to be like. Our tribe turns out not to be quite our tribe. To join it or remain a part of it, we have to suppress something of ourselves, to pretend or risk expulsion, which may be worse.

Coventry, the physical place with its schools and hotels and railway station, isn't the only Coventry, of course. There's another more famous metaphorical one, the Coventry of the phrase "to be sent to Coventry," meaning to be ostracized or shunned, to be treated as if invisible, inaudible. As if nothing. Ghostly. The origin of the phrase is uncertain—the suggestion that it has something to do with Peeping Tom's fate is neat but likely false. Another theory is that it dates back to the English Civil War in the seventeenth century, when Royalist prisoners were sent to the parliamentary stronghold of Coventry. Whatever the etymology, for just a moment at that convention I felt

like a citizen of both Coventrys. Half Asian, half white, all
alone. Nothing to anyone.

Interestingly, from a distance of forty years, I now realize that
Star Trek—the original series (*TOS* to fans), at least—is very
much about loneliness and isolation. Spock's fish-out-of-water,
half-human, half-Vulcan identity is the obvious example (and
one that spoke to me profoundly), but episode after episode
features sole survivors, stranded characters on deserted planets,
lonely figures with only robot or alien companions. Charlie X,
Miri, the Horta, the Doomsday Machine are all left-behinds
or last-of-their-kinds. Even the great villain Khan, with his
band of fanatical followers, is an exile, an outcast.

But it's perhaps not surprising that loneliness should be a
subtext of the show. Space *is* "the final frontier" and *Star Trek*'s
creator, Gene Roddenberry, conceived it as a "wagon train to
the stars." One thing we know about the frontier is that it's a
lonely place. And space, moreover, is vast, a scale against which
anyone would feel lonely.

Yet alongside and in contrast to all these loners and isolates, the show offers several versions of community: some,
like Khan's group, are dangerous (there's a recurring strain of
skepticism about cultish or conformist communities in several
episodes, something that finds its apotheosis in the Borg of
Star Trek: The Next Generation) and some benign, the multi-
racial crew of the *Enterprise* being Exhibit A. It's perhaps that
glimmering hope of community—the ship, the bridge crew,

the trio of friends made up of Kirk, Spock, and McCoy—set against a backdrop of cosmic loneliness that explains some of the show's enduring appeal. Television and books, more generally, are often about loneliness—they're media of loneliness, indeed (unlike theater, or film, or music, which are often socially consumed)—and yet partaking of them individually, privately, in isolation, nonetheless connects us to all those invisible strangers out there who are also watching and reading by themselves.

A lesson of *Star Trek* then, of the *Enterprise*'s crew—paradoxically a balm to my alienation at that convention—may be that we find companionship not with our own, those like us, but with those others, unlike us, even aliens, with whom all we share is a voyage of loneliness. Which sometimes turns out to be enough.

Letting Go

MAYA SHANBHAG LANG

I stare out the kitchen window, unable to focus. It's a gorgeous June day, the sky a brilliant blue, yet I cannot remember the last time I stepped out into the backyard. My fellowship application is due in two days and I am weeks behind.

"Sorry to bother you," my mother says, interrupting my thoughts. She hovers at the threshold. "I was just wondering . . . when am I going home? Can you drive me? Today?" She looks small and frightened.

"Do you mind if I take you in a bit?" I ask. "I'm just finishing up something."

"Oh! Of course." As she shuffles away, I try not to feel guilty.

My mother and I have this conversation daily. It varies only when she accuses me of poisoning or robbing her.

I cannot remind my mother that her doctor deemed it unsafe for her to live alone, so I pretend she is visiting rather than living with me. This is a mercy to us both. Dementia patients don't like to be reminded of their dementia. I have an hour before I need to pick up my seven-year-old daughter from school. If I try to reason with my mother, my time will be squandered. As my mother's full-time caregiver and my daughter's full-time mom, I need to protect my time however possible.

Every day, I remind myself that pretenses are necessary—that it isn't wrong to lie to my mother. I must repeat this to myself over and over, as though I am the one with Alzheimer's.

I am in my thirties, my mother in her sixties. I crave scenes of a doting grandparent who bakes cookies and reads bedtime stories. Instead, I cook my mother's meals, help her into the shower, soothe her when she grows agitated.

I turn back to my laptop. The time passes as it always does, too quickly. Soon I am rushing out the door, aware that the afternoon will whiz by in a blur: helping my daughter with her homework, cobbling together dinner. My husband, after getting home, will want to talk to me about his job, issues with his family, and I will want to listen, to be the good wife, just as I want to be the good mom, the good daughter, all while the fellowship application nags at my thoughts, taunting me for thinking I am good at anything at all.

As I pass the guest room on my way out, I see that my mother is fast asleep, my promise to drive her home long forgotten, as most of my words to her are.

In the mornings, I place a small white pill in the palm of her hand. The pill is Aricept, the leading Alzheimer's medication.

Just a few years ago, my mother ran clinical trials for Aricept.

Back then she would have rattled off its chemical structure and contraindications. I would have been filled with pride for her. Newly divorced at fifty-five, she reinvented herself as a clinical researcher after decades of working as a psychiatrist. She was happier than I had ever seen her. Back then, I did not know how limited our time was—that soon she would be taking the very medication she helped advance. I did not think to tell her how much I admired her, how grateful I was for her, how glad I was when she divorced my father.

As I place the pill in her palm, I want to tell her that she is a formidable scientist, a no-nonsense physician, a force of nature. *You are my mother*, I want to say, though I recognize that the words are for my benefit.

How do we negotiate ambiguous loss? My mother is present but absent. I don't know who I'm talking to, if I should fight for her, try to pull her back to me. She doesn't always want to think about who she once was. It is easier for her to be in the moment, untethered and free—to not face the weight of my expectations. Yet for me, those expectations form the repository of who she was.

I feel caught between past and present. She and I are in the same room, but we are in different times.

She takes the pill, swallows it. Then she shuffles away, her slippered footfalls offering their quiet hush.

"How long can we do this?"

It is winter now. Grudgingly, my mother accepts being

under my care. She eats the food I prepare, allows me to lay out her clothes for the day ahead, but she pesters me with questions.

"I have lived here for a few weeks," she continues sagely. "But how long can this last?" I don't tell her that it's already been several months, that I have no idea how long I can manage, that her question terrifies me.

I tell her what I tell myself: that I'm glad to be able to care for her, that I'm fortunate to have enough space in my house to accommodate her, that I'm lucky to have a flexible career and an understanding husband. I rattle off my memorized gratitude list while cooking, spatula in one hand, phone in the other.

While checking email, I learn that I've been turned down for the fellowship. I cannot say that I'm surprised—it was thrown together in such a rush—but I am bitterly disappointed. For a moment, I see myself, a woman at a stove, stirring at a pot. I do not want to be this woman. I feel the lure of martyrdom, how easy it would be to sacrifice myself. It feels like a dare. *Go ahead*, a little voice urges. *Just give in.*

That night at dinner, while my husband works late, I watch my daughter and my mother at the table. They're like siblings, whispering to each other, giggling conspiratorially. It is lovely to watch their ease. Zoe has no expectations of her grandmother. She accepts her as she is.

Later, when my mother asks, "So when is dinner?" Zoe laughs and says, "We just ate, Grandma!" There is no embarrassment or reproach in her voice. The same sentence from me would sound very different. My mother laughs with her, eyes crinkling at the corners.

Years ago, Zoe spotted a rainbow while we were on vacation. She noticed that she could only see it through her sunglasses. "Without them, it disappears!" she said. This, I decide, is how I will try to view my mother's Alzheimer's: the dark lenses through which certain gifts appear. Perhaps I can learn to be in the moment. If nothing else, I can watch my daughter and my mother together, knowing this is time I will not get back again.

With the approach of spring, I feel increasingly isolated. Friends and family have stopped asking about my situation. To them, the arrangement has normalized. It doesn't feel normal to me, though. Time only makes my situation feel more strange.

My world has narrowed to my role as caregiver.

I orbit around my mother. Even when she is in her room with the door closed, I feel acutely aware of her. I am on edge, waiting for the sound of her shuffling footsteps. I'm distracted when listening to my husband and to my daughter. I feel myself giving them less of my attention because I have so little to give. I cannot remember the last time I thought of myself.

Paradoxically, my mother is easier to care for now. She's thriving. She no longer fights me. She eats whatever I cook. She craves my presence. When I emerge from the bathroom, there she stands, waiting. She relaxes at the sight of me and smiles. This is the reliance I once sought, but I recoil from it.

I want her to fight me, to ask questions, to think she is still in control.

She grows in size, her appetite heartier. She requires new clothes every few months. It reminds me of when Zoe was a baby: stacks of outgrown pants accumulate in the closet. Meanwhile, I peck at my food. At night, I cannot sleep.

My mother and I are trading places. We even trade clothes. I wear her discards as my body shrinks; she graduates into my newly loose pants. She sleeps soundly through the night while I get up and pace. She becomes anxious if I am out of sight for just a few minutes. She reaches for me, hugs me in a way she never did when I was a child.

I do not confide in friends about how I feel. I feel disconnected from them, on the other side of a wall. I haven't applied for any fellowships or teaching positions in almost a year. Why would I? I wouldn't be able to teach a class; I cannot leave the house. I have not written anything new and cannot fathom doing so. All this time, I thought my mother was a shell of herself, but I am the one who feels empty.

This is the problem with seeing the world through dark lenses: Even though there is the occasional rainbow, most of the brightness gets dulled. We forget how life is supposed to look.

Here is what's strange about this time: each day I spend with my mother, I have the disconcerting feeling of losing her more, as though we are both erasing ourselves.

She is letting go of being a mother.

I am letting go of being a daughter.

I wish more than anything that I could engage with her, have a candid conversation, lay out the facts. I want to play the highlight reel that exists in my head, the video montage of evidence to justify my choices. I am seeking forgiveness, I suppose. I am also seeking understanding. I want to tell her that this is hard for me, too, that I have no idea what I'm doing, that I never imagined assuming responsibility for her. I want to confide in her about *her*. I want my former mom to help me with my current one.

Truthfully, I cannot emulate Zoe's acceptance of my mother. I try to, but some part of me holds on, refusing to let go. This part of me will not go away, nor do I want it to. It's the part of me that remembers my mother as she was.

For months, I agonize over whether to move my mother into an assisted living facility. Our situation is untenable, but sending her away is unthinkable. I am convinced she will be miserable. I have become so inured to our situation that my own misery no longer registers.

Taking off the dark sunglasses requires courage. I never imagined becoming my mother's caregiver, but now I cannot imagine life otherwise. I finally give myself permission to let go by telling myself, as I tell her, that she will be there temporarily. Sometimes, a pretext is necessary, even for oneself.

To my surprise, at the assisted living facility my mother

finds what I could not give her: peers, social support, community. When I call her, she has stories of friends and bingo tournaments. She often sounds irked to hear from me, like a college student on her way out the door.

I know now why I felt so miserable, standing at that stove, stirring at that pot. I didn't allow myself to imagine more for myself. I equated prioritizing myself with doom.

This, I think, is the most oppressive feature of loneliness, the way it limits the imagination, whispering to us that life will never be better, that we are not allowed to envision possibilities. Loneliness chips away at the space we occupy.

In my apprehension, I forgot that good outcomes can exist on the other side of uncertainty, that we cannot see the benefits of a new life until we take a leap.

The name for this leap is self-love. Others benefit from it in ways we cannot foresee.

Weeks later, I find myself one afternoon stepping into my backyard. The wisteria has started to bloom, climbing up the side of the house in its wild purple reach.

I turn my face up to the sky. It is a glorious day, the sky a brilliant blue. This is what my mother would have wanted for me, to stand in the light. I know now that when we let go, we do not lose—for in the act of letting go, we find ourselves, come back to ourselves, and this reunion is joyous, exceeding what we once dared imagine.

Trading Stories

JHUMPA LAHIRI

Books, and the stories they contained, were the only things I felt I was able to possess as a child. Even then, the possession was not literal; my father is a librarian, and perhaps because he believed in collective property, or perhaps because my parents considered buying books for me an extravagance, or perhaps because people generally acquired less then than they do now, I had almost no books to call my own. I remember coveting and eventually being permitted to own a book for the first time. I was five or six. The book was diminutive, about four inches square, and was called *You'll Never Have to Look for Friends*. It lived among the penny candy and the Wacky Packs at the old-fashioned general store across the street from our first house in Rhode Island. The plot was trite, more an extended greeting card than a story. But I remember the excitement of watching my mother purchase it for me and of bringing it home. Inside the front cover, beneath the declaration "This book is especially for," was a line on which to write my name. My mother did so, and also wrote the word *mother* to indicate that the book had been given to me by her, though

I did not call her Mother but Ma. "Mother" was an alternate
guardian. But she had given me a book that, nearly forty years
later, still dwells on a bookcase in my childhood room.

Our house was not devoid of things to read, but the offerings felt scant, and were of little interest to me. There were
books about China and Russia that my father read for his graduate studies in political science, and issues of *Time* that he read
to relax. My mother owned novels and short stories and stacks
of a literary magazine called *Desh*, but they were in Bengali,
even the titles illegible to me. She kept her reading material
on metal shelves in the basement, or off-limits by her bedside.
I remember a yellow volume of lyrics by the poet Kazi Nazrul
Islam, which seemed to be a holy text to her, and a thick, fray-
ing English dictionary with a maroon cover that was pulled
out for Scrabble games. At one point, we bought the first few
volumes of a set of encyclopedias that the supermarket where
we shopped was promoting, but we never got them all. There
was an arbitrary, haphazard quality to the books in our house,
as there was to certain other aspects of our material lives. I
craved the opposite: a house where books were a solid presence, piled on every surface and cheerfully lining the walls. At
times, my family's effort to fill our house with books seemed
thwarted; this was the case when my father mounted rods and
brackets to hold a set of olive-green shelves. Within a few days
the shelves collapsed, the Sheetrocked walls of our 1970s-era
Colonial unable to support them.

What I really sought was a better-marked trail of my parents' intellectual lives: bound and printed evidence of what

they'd read, what had inspired and shaped their minds. A connection, via books, between them and me. But my parents did
not read to me or tell me stories; my father did not read any
fiction, and the stories my mother may have loved as a young
girl in Calcutta were not passed down. My first experience of
hearing stories aloud occurred the only time I met my mater-
nal grandfather, when I was two, during my first visit to India.
He would lie back on a bed and prop me up on his chest and
invent things to tell me. I am told that the two of us stayed up
long after everyone else had gone to sleep, and that my grandfather kept extending these stories, because I insisted that they
not end.

Bengali was my first language, what I spoke and heard at
home. But the books of my childhood were in English, and
their subjects were, for the most part, either English or American lives. I was aware of a feeling of trespassing. I was aware
that I did not belong to the worlds I was reading about: that
my family's life was different, that different food graced our
table, that different holidays were celebrated, that my family
cared and fretted about different things. And yet when a book
was in my possession, and as I read it, this didn't matter. I entered into a pure relationship with the story and its characters,
encountering fictional worlds as if physically, inhabiting them
fully, at once immersed and invisible.

In life, especially as a young girl, I was afraid to participate in social activities. I worried about what others might
make of me, how they might judge. But when I read I was
free of this worry. I learned what my fictional companions

ate and wore, learned how they spoke, learned about the toys scattered in their rooms, how they sat by the fire on a cold day drinking hot chocolate. I learned about the vacations they took, the blueberries they picked, the jams their mothers stirred on the stove. For me, the act of reading was one of discovery in the most basic sense—the discovery of a culture that was foreign to my parents. I began to defy them in this way, and to understand, from books, certain things that they didn't know. Whatever books came into the house on my account were part of my private domain. And so I felt not only that I was trespassing but also that I was, in some sense, betraying the people who were raising me.

When I began to make friends, writing was the vehicle. So that, in the beginning, writing, like reading, was less a solitary pursuit than an attempt to connect with others. I did not write alone but with another student in my class at school. We would sit together, this friend and I, dreaming up characters and plots, taking turns writing sections of the story, passing the pages back and forth. Our handwriting was the only thing that separated us, the only way to determine which section was whose. I always preferred rainy days to bright ones, so that we could stay indoors at recess, sit in the hallway, and concentrate. But even on nice days I found somewhere to sit, under a tree or on the ledge of the sandbox, with this friend, and sometimes one or two others, to continue the work on our tale. The stories were transparent riffs on what I was reading at the time:

families living on prairies, orphaned girls sent off to boarding schools or educated by stern governesses, children with supernatural powers, or the ability to slip through closets into alternate worlds. My reading was my mirror, and my material; I saw no other part of myself.

My love of writing led me to theft at an early age. The diamonds in the museum, what I schemed and broke the rules to obtain, were the blank notebooks in my teacher's supply cabinet, stacked in neat rows, distributed for us to write out sentences or practice math. The notebooks were slim, stapled together, featureless, either light blue or a brownish-yellow shade. The pages were lined, their dimensions neither too small nor too large. Wanting them for my stories, I worked up the nerve to request one or two from the teacher. Then, on learning that the cabinet was not always locked or monitored, I began helping myself to a furtive supply.

In the fifth grade, I won a small prize for a story called "The Adventures of a Weighing Scale," in which the eponymous narrator describes an assortment of people and other creatures who visit it. Eventually the weight of the world is too much, the scale breaks, and it is abandoned at the dump. I illustrated the story—all my stories were illustrated back then—and bound it together with bits of orange yarn. The book was displayed briefly in the school library, fitted with an actual card and pocket. No one took it out, but that didn't matter. The validation of the card and pocket was enough. The prize also came with a gift certificate for a local bookstore. As much as I wanted to own books, I was beset by indecision. For hours, it seemed, I wandered the shelves of the store. In the end, I chose a book I'd never heard of, Carl Sandburg's *Rootabaga Stories*. I wanted to love those stories, but their old-fashioned wit eluded me. And yet I kept the book as a talisman, perhaps, of that first recognition. Like the labels on the cakes and bottles that Alice discovers underground, the essential gift of my award was that it spoke to me in the imperative; for the first time, a voice in my head said, "Do this."

As I grew into adolescence and beyond, however, my writing shrank in what seemed to be an inverse proportion to my years. Though the compulsion to invent stories remained, self-doubt began to undermine it, so that I spent the second half of my childhood being gradually stripped of the one comfort I'd known, that formerly instinctive activity turning thorny to the touch. I convinced myself that creative writers were other people, not me, so that what I loved at seven became, by seventeen, the form of self-expression that most intimidated me. I preferred practicing music and performing in plays, learning the notes of a composition or memorizing the lines of a script. I continued working with words, but channeled my energy into essays and articles, wanting to be a journalist. In college, where I studied literature, I decided that I would become an English professor. At twenty-one, the writer in me was like a fly in the room—alive but insignificant, aimless, something that unsettled me whenever I grew aware of it, and which, for the most part, left me alone. I was not at a stage where I needed to worry about rejection from others. My insecurity was systemic, and preemptive, ensuring that, before anyone else had the opportunity, I had already rejected myself.

For much of my life, I wanted to be other people; here was the central dilemma, the reason, I believe, for my creative stasis. I was always falling short of people's expectations: my immigrant parents', my Indian relatives', my American peers', above all my own. The writer in me wanted to edit myself. If only there was a little more this, a little less that, depending on the circumstances: then the asterisk that accompanied me would be removed. My upbringing, an amalgam of two hemispheres, was heterodox and complicated; I wanted it to be conventional and contained. I wanted to be anonymous and ordinary, to look like other people, to behave as others did. To anticipate an alternate future, having sprung from a different past. This had been the lure of acting—the comfort of erasing my identity and adopting another. How could I want to be a writer, to articulate what was within me, when I did not wish to be myself?

It was not in my nature to be an assertive person. I was used to looking to others for guidance, for influence, sometimes for the most basic cues of life. And yet writing stories is one of the most assertive things a person can do. Fiction is an act of willfulness, a deliberate effort to reconceive, to rearrange, to reconstitute nothing short of reality itself. Even among the most reluctant and doubtful of writers, this willfulness must emerge. Being a writer means taking the leap from listening to saying, "Listen to me."

This was where I faltered. I preferred to listen rather than speak, to see instead of be seen. I was afraid of listening to my-self, and of looking at my life.

It was assumed by my family that I would get a PhD. But after I graduated from college, I was, for the first time, no longer a student, and the structure and system I'd known and in some senses depended on fell away. I moved to Boston, a city I knew only vaguely, and lived in a room in the home of people who were not related to me, whose only interest in me was my rent. I found work at a bookstore, opening shipments and running a cash register. I formed a close friendship with a young woman who worked there, whose father is a poet named Bill Corbett. I began to visit the Corbetts' home, which was filled with books and art—a framed poem by Seamus Heaney, drawings by Philip Guston, a rubbing of Ezra Pound's gravestone. I saw the desk where Bill wrote, obscured by manuscripts, letters, and proofs, in the middle of the living room. I saw that the work taking place on this desk was obliged to no one, con-nected to no institution; that this desk was an island, and that Bill worked on his own. I spent a summer living in that house, reading back issues of *The Paris Review* and, when I was alone, in a bright room on the top floor, pecking out sketches and fragments on a typewriter.

I began to want to be a writer. Secretly at first, exchang-ing pages with one other person, our prescheduled meetings forcing me to sit down and produce something. Stealing into the office where I had a job as a research assistant, on weekends and at night, to type stories onto a computer, a machine I did not own at the time. I bought a copy of *Writer's Market*, and sent out stories to little magazines that sent them back to me. The following year, I entered graduate school, not as a writer but as a student of English literature. But beneath my declared scholarly objective there was now a wrinkle. I used to pass a bookshop every day on the way to the train, the storefront displaying dozens of titles that I always stopped to look at. Among them were books by Leslie Epstein, a writer whose work I had not yet read but whose name I knew, as the director of the writing program at Boston University. On a lark one day, I walked into the creative-writing department seeking permission to sit in on a class.

It was audacious of me. The equivalent, nearly two decades later, of stealing notebooks from a teacher's cabinet; of crossing a line. The class was open only to writing students, so I did not expect Epstein to make an exception. After he did, I worked up the nerve to apply for a formal spot in the creative-writing program the following year. When I told my parents that I'd been accepted, with a fellowship, they neither encouraged nor discouraged me. Like so many aspects of my American life, the idea that one could get a degree in creative writing, that it could be a legitimate course of study, seemed perhaps frivolous to them. Still, a degree was a degree, and so their reaction to my decision was to remain neutral. Though I corrected her, my mother, at first, referred to it as a critical-writing program.

My father, I am guessing, hoped it would have something to
do with a PhD.

My mother wrote poems occasionally. They were in Bengali,
and were published now and then in literary magazines in New
England or Calcutta. She seemed proud of her efforts, but she
did not call herself a poet. Both her father and her youngest
brother, on the other hand, were visual artists. It was by their
creative callings that they were known to the world, and had
been described to me. My mother spoke of them reverently. She
told me about the day that my grandfather had had to take his
final exam at the Government College of Art, in Calcutta, and
happened to have a high fever. He was able to complete only a
portion of the portrait he had been asked to render, the subject's
mouth and chin, but it was done so skillfully that he graduated
with honors. Watercolors by my grandfather were brought back
from India, framed, and shown off to visitors, and to this day
I keep one of his medals in my jewelry box, regarding it since
childhood as a good-luck charm.

Before our visits to Calcutta, my mother would make
special trips to an art store to buy the brushes and paper and
pens and tubes of paint that my uncle had requested. Both my
grandfather and my uncle earned their living as commercial
artists. Their fine art brought in little money. My grandfather
died when I was five, but I have vivid memories of my uncle,
working at his table in the corner of the cramped rented apartment where my mother was brought up, preparing layouts for

clients who came to the house to approve or disapprove of his ideas, my uncle staying up all night to get the job done. I gathered that my grandfather had never been financially secure, and that my uncle's career was also precarious—that being an artist, though noble and romantic, was not a practical or responsible thing to do.

Abandoned weighing scales, witches, orphans: these, in childhood, had been my subjects. As a child, I had written to connect with my peers. But when I started writing stories again, in my twenties, my parents were the people I was struggling to reach. In 1992, just before starting the writing program at BU, I went to Calcutta with my family. I remember coming back at the end of summer, getting into bed, and almost immediately writing the first of the stories I submitted that year in workshop. It was set in the building where my mother had grown up, and where I spent much of my time when I was in India. I see now that my impulse to write this story, and several like-minded stories that followed, was to prove something to my parents: that I understood, on my own terms, in my own words, in a limited but precise way, the world they came from. For though they had created me, and reared me, and lived with me day after day, I knew that I was a stranger to them, an American child. In spite of our closeness, I feared that I was alien. This was the predominant anxiety I had felt while growing up.

I was my parents' firstborn child. When I was seven, my mother became pregnant again, and gave birth to my sister in November 1974. A few months later, one of her closest friends in Rhode Island, another Bengali woman, also learned that she was expecting. The woman's husband, like my father, worked at the university. Based on my mother's recommendation, her friend saw the same doctor and planned to deliver at the same hospital where my sister was born. One rainy evening, my parents received a call from the hospital. The woman's husband cried into the telephone as he told my parents that their child had been born dead. There was no reason for it. It had simply happened, as it sometimes does. I remember the weeks following, my mother cooking food and taking it over to the couple, the grief in place of the son who was supposed to have filled their home. If writing is a reaction to injustice, or a search for meaning when meaning is taken away, this was that initial experience for me. I remember thinking that it could have happened to my parents and not to their friends, and I remember, because the same thing had not happened to our family, as my sister was by then a year old already, also feeling ashamed. But, mainly, I felt the unfairness of it—the unfairness of the couple's expectation, unfulfilled.

We moved to a new house, whose construction we had overseen, in a new neighborhood. Soon afterward, the childless couple had a house built in our neighborhood as well. They hired the same contractor, and used the same materials, the same floor plan, so that the houses were practically identical. Other children in the neighborhood, sailing past on bicycles and roller skates, took note of this similarity, finding it funny. I was asked if all Indians lived in matching houses. I resented these children, for not knowing what I knew of the couple's misfortune, and at the same time I resented the couple a little, for having modeled their home on ours, for suggesting that our lives were the same when they were not. A few years later the house was sold, the couple moving away to another town, and an American family altered the facade so that it was no longer a carbon copy of ours. The comic parallel between two Bengali families in a Rhode Island neighborhood was forgotten by the neighborhood children. But our lives had not been parallel; I was unable to forget this.

When I was thirty years old, digging in the loose soil of a new story, I unearthed that time, that first tragic thing I could remember happening, and wrote a story called "A Temporary Matter." It is not exactly the story of what had happened to that couple, nor is it a story of something that happened to me. Springing from my childhood, from the part of me that was slowly reverting to what I loved most when I was young, it was the first story that I wrote as an adult.

My father, who, at eighty, still works forty hours a week at the University of Rhode Island, has always sought security and stability in his job. His salary was never huge, but he supported a family that wanted for nothing. As a child, I did not know the exact meaning of *tenure*, but when my father obtained it I sensed what it meant to him. I set out to do as he had done, and to pursue a career that would provide me with a similar stability and security. But at the last minute I stepped away, because I wanted to be a writer instead. Stepping away was what was essential, and what was also fraught. Even after I received the Pulitzer Prize, my father reminded me that writing stories was not something to count on and that I must always be prepared to earn my living in some other way. I listen to him, and at the same time I have learned not to listen, to wander to the edge of the precipice and to leap. And so, though a writer's job is to look and listen, in order to become a writer I had to be deaf and blind.

I see now that my father, for all his practicality, gravitated toward a precipice of his own, leaving his country and his family, stripping himself of the reassurance of belonging. In reaction, for much of my life, I wanted to belong to a place, either the one my parents came from or America, spread out before us. When I became a writer my desk became home; there was no need for another. Every story is a foreign territory, which, in the process of writing, is occupied and then abandoned. I belong to my work, to my characters, and in order to create new ones I leave the old ones behind. My parents' refusal to let go or to belong fully to either place is at the heart of what I, in a less literal way, try to accomplish in writing. Born of my inability to belong, it is my refusal to let go.

On Witness and Respair

JESMYN WARD

My Beloved died in January. He was a foot taller than me and had large, beautiful dark eyes and dexterous, kind hands. He fixed me breakfast and pots of loose-leaf tea every morning. He cried at both of our children's births, silently, tears glazing his face. Before I drove our children to school in the pale dawn light, he would put both hands on the top of his head and dance in the driveway to make the kids laugh. He was funny, quick-witted, and could inspire the kind of laughter that cramped my whole torso. Last fall, he decided it would be best for him and our family if he went back to school. His primary job in our household was to shore us up, to take care of the children, to be a househusband. He traveled with me often on business trips, carried our children in the back of lecture halls, watchful and quietly proud as I spoke to audiences, as I met readers and shook hands and signed books. He indulged my penchant for Christmas movies, for meandering trips through museums, even though he would have much preferred to be in a stadium somewhere, watching football. One of my favorite places in the world was beside him, under his warm arm, the color of deep, dark river water.

In early January, we became ill with what we thought was flu. Five days into our illness, we went to a local urgent care center, where the doctor swabbed us and listened to our chests. The kids and I were diagnosed with flu; my Beloved's test was inconclusive. At home, I doled out medicine to all of us: Tamiflu and promethazine. My children and I immediately began to feel better, but my Beloved did not. He burned with fever. He slept and woke to complain that he thought the medicine wasn't working, that he was in pain. And then he took more medicine and slept again. Two days after our family doctor visit, I walked into my son's room where my Beloved lay, and he panted: *Can't. Breathe.* I brought him to the emergency room, where after an hour in the waiting room, he was sedated and put on a ventilator. His organs failed: first his kidneys, then his liver. He had a massive infection in his lungs, developed sepsis, and in the end, his great strong heart could no longer support a body that had turned on him. He coded eight times. I witnessed the doctors perform CPR and bring him back four. Within fifteen hours of walking into the emergency room of that hospital, he was dead. The official reason: acute respiratory distress syndrome. He was thirty-three years old.

Without his hold to drape around my shoulders, to shore me up, I sank into hot, wordless grief.

•

Two months later, I squinted at a video of a gleeful Cardi B chanting in a singsong voice: *Coronavirus,* she cackled. *Coronavirus.* I stayed silent while people around me made jokes about COVID, rolled their eyes at the threat of pandemic. Weeks later, my kids' school was closed. Universities were telling students to vacate the dorms while professors were scrambling to move classes online. There was no bleach, no toilet paper, no paper towels for purchase anywhere. I snagged the last of the disinfectant spray off a pharmacy shelf, the clerk ringing up my purchases asking me wistfully, *Where did you find that at,* and for one moment, I thought she would challenge me for it, tell me there was some policy in place to prevent my buying it.

Days became weeks, and the weather was strange for south Mississippi, for the swampy, water-ridden part of the state I call home: low humidity, cool temperatures, clear, sun-lanced skies. My children and I awoke at noon to complete homeschooling lessons. As the spring days lengthened into summer, my children ran wild, exploring the forest around my house, picking blackberries, riding bikes and four-wheelers in their underwear. They clung to me, rubbed their faces into my stomach, and cried hysterically: *I miss Daddy,* they said. Their hair grew tangled and dense. I didn't eat, except when I did, and then it was tortillas, queso, and tequila.

The absence of my Beloved echoed in every room of our house. Him folding me and the children in his arms on our monstrous fake-suede sofa. Him shredding chicken for enchiladas in the kitchen. Him holding our daughter by the hands and pulling her upward, higher and higher, so she floated at the

top of her leap in a long bed-jumping marathon. Him shaving
the walls of the children's playroom with a sander after an
internet recipe for homemade chalkboard paint went wrong:
green dust everywhere.

During the pandemic, I couldn't bring myself to leave the
house, terrified I would find myself standing in the doorway of
an ICU room, watching the doctors press their whole weight
on the chest of my mother, my sisters, my children, terrified
of the lurch of their feet, the lurch that accompanies each press
that restarts the heart, the jerk of their pale, tender soles, terrified of the frantic prayer without intention that keens through
the mind, the prayer for life that one says in the doorway, the
prayer I never want to say again, the prayer that dissolves mid-
air when the hush-click-hush-click of the ventilator drowns
it, terrified of the terrible commitment at the heart of me that
reasons that if the person I love has to endure this, then the
least I can do is stand there, the least I can do is witness, the
least I can do is tell them over and over again, aloud, *I love you.
We love you. We ain't going nowhere.*

As the pandemic settled in and stretched, I set my alarms to
wake early, and on mornings after nights where I actually
slept, I woke and worked on my novel in progress. The novel
is about a woman who is even more intimately acquainted
with grief than I am, an enslaved woman whose mother is
stolen from her and sold south to New Orleans, whose lover
is stolen from her and sold south, who herself is sold south and

descends into the hell of chattel slavery in the mid-1800s. My loss was a tender second skin. I shrugged against it as I wrote, haltingly, about this woman who speaks to spirits and fights her way across rivers.

My commitment surprised me. Even in a pandemic, even in grief, I found myself commanded to amplify the voices of the dead that sing to me, from their boat to my boat, on the sea of time. On most days, I wrote one sentence. On some days, I wrote one thousand words. Many days, it and I seemed useless. All of it, misguided endeavor. My grief bloomed as depression, just as it had after my brother died at nineteen, and I saw little sense, little purpose in this work, this solitary vocation. Me, sightless, wandering the wild, head thrown back, mouth wide open, singing to a star-drenched sky. Like all the speaking, singing women of old, a maligned figure in the wilderness. Few listened in the night.

What resonated back to me: The emptiness between the stars. Dark matter. Cold.

Did you see it? my cousin asked me.

No. I couldn't bring myself to watch it, I said. Her words began to flicker, to fade in and out. Grief sometimes makes it hard for me to hear. Sound came in snatches.

His knee, she said.

On his neck, she said.

Couldn't breathe, she said.

He cried for his mama, she said.

I read about Ahmaud, I said. *I read about Breonna.*

I didn't say, but I thought it: *I know their beloveds' wail. I know their beloveds' wail. I know their beloveds wander their pandemic rooms, pass through their sudden ghosts. I know their loss burns their beloveds' throats like acid. Their families will speak*, I thought. *Ask for justice. And no one will answer*, I thought. *I know this story: Trayvon, Tamir, Sandra.*

Cuz, I said, *I think you told me this story before.*

I think I wrote it.

I swallowed sour.

In the days after my conversation with my cousin, I woke to people in the streets. I woke to Minneapolis burning. I woke to protests in America's heartland, Black people blocking the highways. I woke to people doing the haka in New Zealand. I woke to hoodie-wearing teens, to John Boyega raising a fist in the air in London, even as he was afraid he would sink his career, but still, he raised his fist. I woke to droves of people, masses of people in Paris, sidewalk to sidewalk, moving like a river down the boulevards. I knew the Mississippi. I knew the plantations on its shores, the movement of enslaved and cotton up and down its eddies. The people marched, and I had never known that there could be rivers such as this, and as protesters chanted and stomped, as they grimaced and shouted and groaned, tears burned my eyes. They glazed my face.

I sat in my stuffy pandemic bedroom and thought I might never stop crying. The revelation that Black Americans were not alone in this, that others around the world believed that Black Lives Matter broke something in me, some immutable belief I'd carried with me my whole life. This belief beat like another heart—*thump*—in my chest from the moment I took my first breath as an underweight, two-pound infant after my mother, ravaged by stress, delivered me at twenty-four weeks. It beat from the moment the doctor told my Black mother her Black baby would die. *Thump.*

That belief was infused with fresh blood during the girl-hood I'd spent in underfunded public school classrooms, cavities eating away at my teeth from government-issued block cheese, powdered milk, and cornflakes. *Thump.* Fresh blood in the moment I heard the story of how a group of white men, revenue agents, had shot and killed my great-great-grandfather, left him to bleed to death in the woods like an animal, from the second I learned no one was ever held accountable for his death. *Thump.* Fresh blood in the moment I found out the white drunk driver who killed my brother wouldn't be charged for my brother's death, only for leaving the scene of the car accident, the scene of the crime. *Thump.*

This is the belief that America fed fresh blood into for centuries, this belief that Black lives have the same value as a plow horse or a grizzled donkey. I knew this. My family knew this. My people knew this, and we fought it, but we were convinced we would fight this reality alone, fight until we could

no more, until we were in the ground, bones moldering, head-
stones overgrown above in the world where our children and
children's children still fought, still yanked against the noose,
the forearm, the starvation and redlining and rape and enslavement and murder and choked out: *I can't breathe.* They would
say: *I can't breathe. I can't breathe.*

I cried in wonder each time I saw a protest around the
world because I recognized the people. I recognized the way
they zipped their hoodies, the way they raised their fists, the
way they walked, the way they shouted. I recognized their ac-
tion for what it was: witness. Even now, each day, they witness.

They witness injustice.

They witness this America, this country that gaslighted us
for four hundred fucking years.

Witness that my state, Mississippi, waited until 2013 to rat-
ify the Thirteenth Amendment.

Witness that Mississippi didn't remove the Confederate
battle emblem from its state flag until 2020.

Witness Black people, Indigenous people, so many poor
brown people, lying on beds in frigid hospitals, gasping our
last breaths with COVID-riddled lungs, rendered flat by undiagnosed underlying conditions, triggered by years of food
deserts, stress, and poverty, lives spent snatching sweets so we
could eat one delicious morsel, savor some sugar on the tongue,
oh Lord, because the flavor of our lives is so often bitter.

They witness our fight too, the quick jerk of our feet, see
our hearts lurch to beat again in our art and music and work
and joy. How revelatory that others witness our battles and

stand up. They go out in the middle of a pandemic, and they march.

I sob, and the rivers of people run in the streets.

When my Beloved died, a doctor told me: *The last sense to go is hearing. When someone is dying, they lose sight and smell and taste and touch. They even forget who they are. But in the end, they hear you.*

I hear you.

I hear you.

You say:

I love you.

We love you.

We ain't going nowhere.

I hear you say:

We here.

Reliquary: A Quartet

LIDIA YUKNAVITCH

1. Nest

A tiny hummingbird's nest sits on my blood-red writing desk. The nest was a gift, beloved to me, and yet every time I look at it I ask myself, What happened to the hummingbirds? Were they finished with the small home? Were they displaced? Did the nest fall when the hummingbirds left, or was the nest invaded? Did some other creature kill them and eat them? Or is the absence marked by flight and becoming? Death or life?

It's a question that haunts me even as the nest-gift is filled with aura to me. I am a lover of solitary objects, particularly organic objects: bones, hair, nests, animal skulls, feathers, rocks, shells, petals. Everything of life that it once held, the tiny hearts beating, the small wings fluttering, the hovering of it all, now untraceable but for bits of minuscule feather fluff woven here and there into a cup along with plant down, bark, lichen, leaf matter, and spider silk. The empty nest is either a delicate and beautiful artifact from the natural word or a stain, a violence.

The emptiness.

Hummingbirds select sheltered locations for building nests. Dense or thorny shrubs. The forked branch of a tree. The locations that intrigue me the most include those balanced on wires or Christmas lights. On top of porch lamps or security cameras. Inside basketball nets, on top of wind chimes, ceiling sprinklers, the very top of a cactus. What formidable imaginations—to choose such unusual shelter spots. The nests are built solely by the female bird. She chooses the nesting sites, gathers the materials, raises the babies. She spends several hours a day for seven days collecting materials in a kind of frenzy.

Then she does something unusual.

She holds still.

2. *Miles*

In the fall of 2019 I had the deep privilege of being the writer-in-residence at a college in rural upstate New York. The job involved nine months on-site where I taught one creative writing seminar two days a week.

The rest of the time was mine.

That sentence had never happened to me before in my life.

The gift of alone. For nine months.

When I say alone, what I mean is my husband stayed home in Oregon that year to help our son make the transition from high school to college. Had I stayed home that year with them, I would have had to face my son's leaving for college too. A normal transitional phase, right?

I am not lying to you when I say I thought it might kill me. I started talking to anyone who would listen about my dread and sadness about my son leaving home to go to college. No really, ask around. There are probably people who will read this who remember how many years I talked about my son's pending departure. I'd cry talking about it. Many women and men were compassionate with me; they'd put their hands on my shoulder and ask, "When does your son leave for college?" And I'd have to confess, "In five years." Or four. Or three. Or two. Then one. They'd look at me with concern or something like pity. Who does that? Mourns the loss before it even happens?

I'll tell you who. I was mourning my son's leaving before it ever happened because I carry loss inside my chest where a heart should be. My body is a lifedeath space. My daughter died the day she was born, years ago now. Instead of withstanding the moment of my son's leaving, I moved into that beautiful writer house provided by an esteemed private college over two thousand miles away.

I understand the depth of privilege this opportunity afforded me, even though nothing like this had ever happened to me in my life until that moment; my jam prior to this gig was teaching at a community college for eighteen years, teaching in correctional facilities, and then founding a writing space for people who can't go to college at all. I get it. I know how lucky I have been. Boohoo, you scored a visiting writer job and your son ascended to college seemingly effortlessly.

Ascensions.

Perhaps because I was raised Catholic for a while growing up, or perhaps because I've spent my entire adult life force endeavoring to help people who get shoved to the margins grow wings, the first thing I felt was irrepressible guilt: a sticky, thick, and putrid guilt that oozes like too-old blood that got stuck in some mother-daughter wound.

I puzzled on that guilt. Should I turn this job down? Money and time, two things I only knew how to scrap for. Wasn't the scrap and hustle more important than the opportunity? Wasn't I just another white woman jackass if I took this opportunity? Then I realized my ego was just doing some kind of slippery dance . . . *Fuck that*, I thought. *That guilt is useless and just another tricky form of privilege. Quit having false fluttery frenzied battles with yourself and suck it up. This chance won't come again. Ever. You are not more righteous if you are in love with your own scrap and struggle than you are with your own possibility.*

The next thing I felt was unworthy. It is not a lie to say I know hundreds of writers who are more talented than I am, whose work lifts me out of bed and keeps me from giving up or in every goddamn day of my life. Some of them are famous. Some are not. Some have yet to publish. None of that matters. What matters is the fact of their words coming alive on pages in spite of the world. The heart and art of them. So I thought to myself, *Get the fuck over yourself. Honor all of those writers you love by being present inside the great storytelling rivers that lead to an ocean bigger than all of us. Step up, woman. Hold the space for whoever comes next. And do what you always do when you are let in a door of privilege: jam your foot in there, agitate, see how you can inspire youngsters to Fuck. Shit. Up.*

That's how I came to embrace the alone.

On the first night of my night in a house not mine, I took off my clothes, turned off all the lights, and took the hottest bath of my life, the bathroom window like an eye directly on the moon.

Inside the alone, a grief bird freed herself.

3. Hold

Never let anyone tell you your grief is an emptiness.

There is an alone inside grief, and it is yours, and the alone is both unbearable and simultaneously beautiful. Never let anyone tell you how long your grief should last or what to do with it.

I have spent whole decades inside grief.

I have spent whole decades inside an alone, whether or not there were any people around.

Sometimes inside the alone a story emerges.

In this story there is a grief bird girl, I think maybe with a red head and a black mask, her body gray and white.

Inside this alone story there is a woman with one wing for an arm. The wing is gray and missing some important feathers. The wing is heavy with age and flight. Due to the wing, the woman has only been able to use one of her arms, one of her hands to write.

When I say my grief lifted, I mean that it grew wings and took flight, exactly like a tiny and fierce hummingbird leaving a nest.

The beginning of the story happened already on these pages. It was briefly fluttering in front of you. Did you see it?

Night.

Water.

Moon.

Window.

Bird.

Body.

Write.

The first night alone in the house I turned off all the lights and ran a very hot bath. Our bathtub at home sucks and our water doesn't ever get hot, just like every house or apartment I've ever inhabited. We live in an old bohemian-ish craftsman-style house in the shitty end of not-quite-Portland . . . something is always breaking down or rusting away or just not quite working right, and I'm a terrible housecleaner, but the house is filled with love and art, so who gives a fuck?

And feathers. I collect single feathers.

Anyway, this endless hot water and a functioning bathtub—this was an *epic* moment for me. Plus the bathroom was bigger than some apartments I lived in. When I was sitting in the bathtub alone in the house in the dark the first night, an unusual feeling came forward and filled my entire body. One I had not prepared for. Eyes closed. Hot water all around my body. Tub like a perfect percaline cup around me. The comfort and ease of darkness and peoplelessness only available inside a deep, dark, perfect alone. Which is how it occurred to me.

My pleasure.

The pleasure of a woman whose children—one who died, one who grew—are gone, a woman whose blood has come back to her forever.

I put my hand to the other mouth of me there in the water. I parted the lips of a self. With one finger two fingers I entered myself, the cave of my being, the lifedeath space. With my heavy wing hand, I pounded my clit. The water became waves. My body the waves. My eyes were closed but I recognized the heat surge of my I rising in my hips and cunt.

At the moment of my I coming, I heard a bird outside the night window, I don't know what kind of bird but it had a red head and a black mask and a gray-and-white breast, and the moon was there and she swallowed the bird into her.

4. Writing

At the end of the nine mine-alone months in upstate New York, I returned home to Portland. My son returned home to Portland from college too, because of COVID. So the cleaving was softened into a humming sound. I am not ashamed to admit his coming home elated me, though I try to act casual around it, I try not to hover too near every nanosecond, I try not to flutter my heart against his so hard I leave a bruise or a stain.

I try to hold still.

My husband said the hardest thing about our being gone was the emptiness of the house and how his heart felt away from his body.

One day when I was on a walk with my son, we were on a neighborhood walk—I bet we all know our own neighborhoods more intimately by now than we knew we didn't—I saw a frenzied blur out of the corner of my eye.

A white hummingbird. Leucistic, not albino, because its eyes, feet, and bill were black. I pulled that universal parent move where I threw my arm against Miles's chest to stop him, even though he is over six feet tall. I pointed to the bird. I could hear us breathing against our COVID masks one second two seconds three seconds—and then the hummingbird was gone. We walked home wondering what, if anything, it meant.

Each year hummingbirds travel on two migrations. One north, one south. The migrations can span hundreds of thousands of miles. Some can fly up to five hundred miles without stopping. Hummingbirds can fly on every axis. Research indicates that hummingbirds can travel as many as twenty-five miles in one day.

They beat their wings up to eighty times a second, which creates the soft humming sound.

I think the nest on my desk carries the trace of a mother's labor.

I think the emptiness carries the fullness of her life, how she has to keep moving in order to become, how her sexuality returns to her, how she can bring it back to life with her hands.

I think the emptiness of the nest is like my mother-gut, that space that held grief and death and life and joy, now filled with fat and thriving stories.

The Ugly Corner

DINA NAYERI

As a child, I was part of a watery village of rivers, creeks, and aqueducts, a lush haven where every meal saw twenty adults gathered around a *sofreh* for hours of storytelling, feasting, and laughter. My parents were medical doctors in nearby Isfahan. When we weren't visiting my father's rural family, we lived in a modern city house, which was quirky and imaginative, like us. A tree grew through our living room. We had rugs that my grandmother had woven on a real Nain loom. On our walls hung etchings by artists that we knew. Our home had a spirit, and a history. But there was always a room to hide our embarrassing things, our ugly things. Everyone has that, right? The unfinished room where you keep your wonky handicrafts and Super Saver coupons, or tuck away the drunk uncle, or hide evidence of your budding apostasy from the theocracy that's hijacked your country. It's the dark corner, the spot of shame, or lack, that gives a home its secrets.

Then we became refugees, and home, with all its joys and disgraces, vanished.

After sixteen months, first as undocumented immigrants,

then asylum seekers in a camp, we arrived in Oklahoma. Over the years, we moved through a series of smaller and smaller apartments, in a complex for those who had lost their way, drug addicts, teenage mothers. I learned to do without friends. In times of need, you couldn't have a friend; you could only be the recipient of somebody's charity, an object of their pity. So, the thing to do was to toil, to study and exercise and achieve, so that you could get the hell out of there and get back some equal footing. Then, and only then, could you hope for a friend.

In high school I didn't go to parties. I sat on the periphery of a group of girls for lunch. I didn't talk to anybody on the phone after school. But then I got into Princeton, and I was a social creature again. I wasn't the only financial aid kid, and I could hide that part with two campus jobs and a few items from Ann Taylor. All through my twenties, I was flush with friendship, with love. I married. My creativity began to bloom. I had fixed it, I told myself. I got rid of the grime and lack. No more struggling to show that I was smart despite an accent, that I was a child of doctors. No one would ever again catch me hiding a rip in my skirt or erasing used workbooks.

By 2010, I was living in an apartment overlooking the Amstel River, with a husband who had been my best friend in college, a fellow foreign kid in America. Now he was in finance. He wore tailored suits and floppy hair and people called him "continental"—which, in Amsterdam, is what you want, I

guess? I craved to be a writer, to float among interesting people, never taking root. I wanted my dirty old jeans, and enough
cash for haircuts and one cappuccino a day—everything else
was dispensable. But Philip kept talking about "giving me a
life." He kept throwing away my broken-in things and ordering me bougie items his mother might wear.

In years past, we had fought. "We met at Princeton," I'd
say. "You didn't rescue me from downtown Kabul. I have my
own ambitions, and clothes aren't it." Now we were largely
silent. We did our own thing and worked on being kinder. We
each had one sad image of the other embedded in our psyche,
and that made us contort to make the other happy: He imagined me sleeping under bridges, unable to survive without him.
I imagined him huddled in a bathtub, alone and friendless.

Although I was afraid of tying myself to one city, Philip
decided that it was time to buy a place. Days after the purchase,
he hired his boss's decorator and told me to "help Sander." So
I did, though it was never my home. It was designer and ster-
ile, good for a couple of thirtysomethings who'd spent their
twenties drifting through hotels. It had seventeen windows—I
remember that number because, instead of writing my book,
I kept multiplying fabric widths and prices by seventeen.

After a while, though, I started to look forward to Sander's
visits. He was blond and joyful and flamboyantly gay in a way
that seemed a part of his brand: he understood that Amsterdam's finance bros considered this the source of his creativity.
And he was warm, with a leather satchel and inexplicably yellow teeth that made me trust him (how easily he wore this

flaw). Besides, he wouldn't judge; he was there to fix what de-
fects he found. We shopped for couches, visited antique shops,
ate roast beef sandwiches. We were equally thrilled by turning
ordinary things into art, and since it wasn't *my* money, Sander
saw that he could share the humble origins of some of the
items. He would text me photos of junk in his storage unit
and say things like "I'm going to frame these finger puppets
for your hallway." Or "What if we turn this old baby kimono
into a painting?" I told him about my first novel, how afraid
I was. He said, "This is the best moment for you. Right now,
it could be the most successful book in the history of books!"
Privately, I found the end result of his decorating too pristine.
The apartment had no secret places, no ugly corners—every
room gleamed. Yet Sander and Philip considered that a feature, and I dismissed my every instinct. Then, overnight, the
last blind was hung and Sander went away, and I felt ashamed
that I had thought we were friends.

I attended Philip's work functions, where the wives talked
about handbags and vacations and suggested I upgrade my
watch. I joined the American Women's Club, where the
women spent long afternoons playing mah-jongg and discuss-
ing gardening solutions. I joined a book club, where we read
treacly bestsellers and rehashed the plot. I drank heavily to
keep my mouth shut and threw up in my square toilet.

Every morning I woke up alone in my big bed and looked
up at the baby kimono. I stood under a waterfall and examined

my body. Nobody had seen me naked in months. One morning, I found a box of expired birth control pills. Did I used to take these? I must have. I lived in a fog.

I passed my days writing in cafés. In the evenings, I bought a special item: a mango, or a KitKat for after dinner. Sometimes Philip ate at home. Sometimes he didn't. I forgot my ambitions for a while, letting myself be subsumed in his.

On weekends I'd walk the canals, watch clusters of people eating and drinking, and wish one of them would pull me into their circle. If I found that first thread, I thought, I could pull until I unraveled the city.

Meanwhile, that September I quietly applied to the Iowa Writers' Workshop, thousands of miles away.

One evening, as I was watching television and slicing my mango, I thought maybe I need an activity, like the kind that kept me busy in college. I started googling combinations of words: *books, Americans, friends, social, research, academic.* What kept coming up was the Fulbright Program. Every year around twenty Fulbrights arrived from America, every one of them bookish, young, and totally alone. I wrote to the director, offering a self-conscious and needlessly boastful introduction, saying that I missed mentoring, and perhaps I could be useful to the Fulbrights. Somehow it was decided I would visit the Fulbrights' orientation meeting to invite them to biweekly dinners at my place.

That weekend, I gleefully purchased cookware for twenty.

I bought a restaurant-sized stewpot, bowls, big spoons, beer glasses. I imagined cold evenings with soup. I looked at the stony white couches Sander and I had picked out together and thought of how cozy they'd look cradling fifteen bodies watching a movie, drinking beers.

On the morning of the orientation, I put on a skirt and blouse, blew out my hair, smeared on lip gloss, then wiped it off. After a curt Dutch intro, the director invited me forward. The fellows glanced at one another. I cleared my throat and started in on my credentials. I'm not sure how much I said before I got to the point: "Basically, I live in a big empty apartment . . . and maybe you guys want to come round to dinner sometimes? I have a . . . huge soup pot." I felt so stupid. But there was a nod, two or three kind smiles, a handsome face, an excited one, a woman from the Middle East, and at least two men that looked like they came from the South, a place like Oklahoma where I had grown up. And every single one of them seemed psyched for free food.

The first night I cooked three Iranian dishes. I needed the massive pot for all three, so I started in the morning, cooked lamb with herbs, scrubbed the pot and cooked beef with egg- plant, then scrubbed the pot again and cooked vegan lentil stew. I made buttery rice pilaf. I showered and fixed my hair. All of the Fulbrights came, and so did Philip. At first, they were curious about me and my reasons for inviting them. But then they had a beer, then two; it was just an ordinary party, and I wondered why I had spent so much time worrying. I spoke to the Middle Eastern woman, Miriam. She asked about home and I told her about our escape from Iran, about living in refugee camps, about struggling to get into Princeton, then meeting Philip. She smiled.

Why was I so afraid of people coming into this ideal home, seeing this sparkling life? I wasn't a refugee anymore. I wasn't counting change. This was the life I had struggled for. This was the "when" that I meant when I whispered to myself that "I can have friends *when* the footing is equal, *when* no one is doing any favors, *when* there is no pity to be felt." Was I still impoverished somehow? Was there some filthy corner I had missed, as I was draping all those windows?

Two weeks later, I cooked up another feast. The Fulbrights returned with bottles of wine and hung out until the early hours. As I checked everyone's drinks, I noticed two of them flirting. I felt powerful, like I had created their spark and made this loving moment possible.

Philip excused himself early for bed. When the last tram came and went, I grabbed five pairs of Philip's Brooks Brothers pajamas and made beds for the stragglers on the couch and the living room floor. Their presence warmed me as I prepared for bed. Our chilly home was full of people breathing, dreaming. The next morning, I woke up alone, to the buzz of my phone. "Why is our living room full of strangers in my pajamas!" Philip said.

"They aren't strangers," I said. "You've met them twice."

"I almost tripped over one," he said. Then he calmed. "Can you please just throw them in the washer so I have some tonight?" He sounded so sad.

"I'm just trying to . . ."

"I know," he said. "Love you."

One night, Angela (from my writing group) and I decided to
bake hashish cupcakes. She had since joined one of my writing
groups, and I wanted to try it, this drug that had wrecked the
lives of so many Iranians. Maybe it would help me feel happier, or more certain. We mixed the hash into melted butter. It
smelled pungent and earthy, so we mixed in peanut butter and
frosted the cupcakes with raspberry jelly.

An hour after our first cupcake, I started to panic. I locked
myself in the bathroom, taking careful note of everything. I
kept thinking I'd humiliate myself: walk out with my pants
unzipped or the toilet unflushed. But mostly that entire hash
trip was a struggle not to talk. Angela kept trying to get me
to relax and open up to her, to tell my stories. Somehow,
though, her efforts felt like an interrogation—what was she
trying to find out? Was she a spy? Was she from the Iranian
government? Where were my passports? Oh my god, where
are the passports? What if she was from the American em-
bassy, checking in to make sure I'm still a worthy American?
Come to think of it, her Fulbright project sounded super
phony—she was studying pirates. Literally. *Pirates.* Oh my
god, it was just like the Islamic Republic to send a blond
Germanic hipster with a pirate fetish to kidnap or assassinate
me. They chose that so they could mock me in Evin Prison.
It's such an Iranian trick, to concoct a situation so they could

say, "Look at her, miss hotshot American, thinks they give PhDs in pirate!"

Or maybe Angela was someone more like those reality show producers, who pretend to care but are out to make you humiliate yourself. I used to watch those shows and hold back the panic each time someone thought they were being vulnerable, or sweet, or honest, or real, and what they were really being was ridiculous. I ran out of the bathroom holding my head.

"What's wrong?" said Angela. "I can't," I said. I kept saying it, "I can't . . . every thought . . . I can't hold on to thoughts." She helped me breathe, then told me to try to stand on one leg and touch my nose. I kept wobbling to one side. We started laughing. Once you start laughing, she said, that's it. The thing about this drug is that whatever feeling you invite runs away with you. So, you have to start laughing before the scary thoughts come.

What had happened to my twenties?

Stop.

What was I doing in Amsterdam?

No!

Why did I marry someone? I'm not a wife.

Shit.

Oh look, I'm a flamingo!

At some point in the evening, I told Angela about the reality show stars, the ones who think they're being honest and vulnerable. "But you know which ones are more embarrassing?" she said. "The ones who think they're hiding something."

•

That February, I got a call from an Iowa number. It was Sam Chang inviting me to join the Writers' Workshop, thousands of miles away. It was time to clean up this overlooked, brambly wing of my life, to read and write and talk to people who wanted the same things, and to fill the spaces where I had once been impoverished. In workshop, one of the first things we learned was to trust our readers. They already know everything. You can't hide or shock or surprise. Allow the story to unfold, without coyness. The things your characters wish most to hide are the very things they're projecting all the time. So, you're free, as a writer, to take down all that scaffolding, to let all the secrets and unspoken indignities show themselves.

Not long ago, Miriam wrote me with her impressions of our time in Amsterdam and the strange way we became friends. Whatever secrets she saw, she wasn't digging for my ugliness. And yet, we were two women from the Middle East who shared so many obsessions. We were both afraid to discuss them, until years later. "I remember you seemed somewhat reckless," she said, "the kind of reckless that comes from being desperately unhappy . . . I think on more than one occasion, I have described you as 'the most ambitious woman I know' and that your ambition frightened me a bit. It seemed born out of a deep desire to prove your worthiness."

In May we threw one last dinner party. We held it out on the street and invited the neighbors, the Fulbrights, Sander, and my writing group. It was Cinco de Mayo and we made margaritas and sopaipillas and real tacos. I looked around and thought of all the pasts that had converged to give this night its flavors: not just Iran, Oklahoma, Princeton, and Amsterdam, but all the places where my guests had lived, where they had found their own hidden back rooms. Halfway through the night, I caught Angela telling Philip a story about a pirate whose case she found in the International Criminal Court in the Hague. "Of course, the ICC!" he said. "I admit I was confused by your thesis topic." They laughed together and he refilled her glass.

Soon this chapter would be over; I would move to Iowa alone and start a life better suited to me. Maybe then, to make things easier, I'd cook a big dinner, invite everyone, and show them my most terrifying thing first. I'd swing open the door to the apostasy room or coupon closet or the drunk uncle, and say, "Here's the place I keep my broken things. Now you can stay or go."

I didn't do that, of course. With each chapter, a new dark corner appears, and each is humiliating in its own surprising way. A decade later, I still say, "Next time, I'll be brave."

Notes from the Midpoint of a Celibate Year

MELISSA FEBOS

There is this woman on my flight to London. I see her, four rows behind me—tousled hair in a wool beanie, leather boots belonging to the category worn only by lesbians and Dickensian orphans, giant backpack—and my seduction sonar locks on to her. Like an insect whose physiology makes its carapace glow during mating season, or the Callery pear trees that emit their volatile amine to attract pollinating insects—thus perfuming my whole Brooklyn street with the ammoniac scent so reminiscent of semen—I feel myself begin to glow with some chemistry visible only to the object of my attention. I don't understand the biological protocol that enacts once it is triggered, but I do know that more often than not, if I want it to be, the end result is sex, and given my history, probably some sort of romantic entanglement.

I cannot say why, six months into my avowed celibacy, I have yielded to the familiar siren song of a cute dyke. I have disengaged myself so many times now from equally compelling opportunities—that editor at the fancy book party, the trans film director, all the loose ends and rain checks with whom I'd cut off contact months ago—but here I am, turning my profile to the angle mathematically most likely for her to see me, rolling my shirt cuffs up to bear a few inches of forearm tattoos, dangling my hand with its short unvarnished nails into the aisle.

Like most femmes, I am an expert at signaling my queerness through physical clues legible only to other queers. I can communicate my sexual identity through the set of my shoulders, if need be. This is all behavior I've largely abstained from over the last six months, but I reason that there is little danger of a full relapse, given that we are on a flight to London and unlikely to come any closer to each other than the four rows of seats now between us.

I am flying to London primarily to meet a gay male friend with whom I will travel to Southampton, where we will board the *Queen Mary 2*, bound for the port of Brooklyn. My friend is taking the *QM2* because he is conducting research in Europe for his new book and he suffers from a debilitating phobia of plane travel. I have agreed to join him because the travel section of a major newspaper has offered to pay the hefty ticket fare in exchange for an essay about my experience on the famed luxury cruise liner. I have taken the opportunity to spend a week in London before our departure to meet with my UK publisher and explore the city.

After we land at London Gatwick, the attractive stranger gathers her belongings, runs a hand through her messy hair, and, yes, glances in my direction, before she rises to her feet and steps into the aisle.

The past six months, to my great surprise, have been the happiest of my life. It wasn't happiness, exactly, that I sought when I decided to spend three months celibate. I was so tired, and I wanted to make better choices. I met my first girlfriend when I was fifteen years old and spent the next twenty years in relationships. I was mostly a serial monogamist, though the ends of many of my affairs overlapped slightly with the beginnings of the ones that followed, forming a kind of daisy chain of romances. There were a few periods of singleness, but I was never *alone*, really. There was always a cohort of flirtations, a string of dates, a lover from my past eager to step into the present, and after a few weeks or months, I'd find my next soul mate.

Once I reached my thirties, I started having moments of unease when I contemplated this pattern. I was just a *relationship person*, I told myself. I took comfort in the fact that I had spent my happiest times partnered, without noting the givenness of that, since I'd spent most of my life partnered. I was reassured by the fact that I never *felt* afraid to be alone. I never considered how one might not ever feel the thing that she had successfully outrun.

Then, at thirty-two, I started a long-distance relationship with a powerfully charismatic woman. For a month or two, it was a surreal exercise in romantic wish fulfillment, as if I were

living in a pop song or a poem. What followed were the most
harrowing two years of my life. I am still hesitant to use the
word *abuse*, though I have not found a better word for what
kept me in that torturous thrall. I had been addicted to heroin
and gotten clean in my twenties, but quitting this woman was
even harder. On the other side of that experience, as I began
to repair my life and all of my other relationships, I understood
that it was time for a reckoning within myself, and I needed
space to do that.

The first few weeks of celibacy were challenging, as I
pruned all romantic prospects from my life and learned to let
opportunities pass. But after that, something incredible happened. My life opened up, like a mansion whose rooms had
been locked. There was so much more space in which to live!
From the long, wordless mornings and days spent at my desk to
quiet evenings of reading in bed, I luxuriated in the solitude. It
was sometimes lonely, but that, too, was novel, like a weather
system that moved through me and after a day, or sometimes
just an hour in the late afternoon as the light changed toward
evening, it moved on. At the end of the three months, I decided on three more. At the end of six months, three more.

The customs line is interminable—the booths woefully un-
derstaffed for the number of incoming passengers—but I'm
distracted entirely by the inching undulation of the line as it
snakes forward, delivering us past each other by mere feet at
regular intervals. Both of us are studiously rotating between

staring at our phones, squinting ahead at the front of the line, and posing in such subtle affectations that no casual observer would discern anything other than boredom and frustration in either of our comportments.

It might seem arrogant for me to assume that my airplane crush reciprocates my attention, but trust me that when you've been performing this choreography for more than twenty years, you know when your partner feels the music and when she doesn't. The thrill, of course, resides in the slender possibility that this time, *this time*, after an unerring decade or so (the first ten years were spent being humiliatingly mistaken a good portion of the time, while I cultivated this precise radar), I might be wrong.

She reaches the booth ten or fifteen people ahead of me and despite devoting a valorous twelve minutes to backpack reorganization and another three to tightening her shoelaces, she is left no other option but to continue on her journey. My disappointment as she disappears into the airport is matched by relief. The spell is broken. I have not violated my abstinence. I dig my passport out of my jacket's interior pocket and shuffle forward, happily bored.

Soon after I got sober at twenty-three, my sponsor told me I couldn't steal anymore. She probably would have told me this sooner, if she'd known that I was still stealing things—mostly books from the Barnes and Noble in Union Square and bags of food from the self-serve bins at the overpriced health food store on University—but I'd never mentioned it, until I happened to be on the phone with her as I walked to my building's laundry room and found that someone had left a stack of quarters on the table by the change machine. *I can take them, right?* I asked her. *Absolutely not*, she said. *We don't steal.*

At the time, I wondered why I had even mentioned it, but now I understand perfectly. I wanted to stop. When she told me to stop, I felt awash in relief. I used to get a terrible wave of anxiety and dread right before I stole, as if someone were making me do it. I hated stealing. When it came to certain objects or stores, once I saw an opportunity, I felt compelled to do it, but it was always stressful to a degree that was never matched by the sense of accomplishment afterward. I wasn't addicted to stealing, but it was a habit I had gotten into as an active addict who wanted to spend every cent that crossed my palm on drugs. It hadn't occurred to me that I could give myself permission to stop.

Incredibly, after I have navigated the swarmed airport, retrieved my massive suitcase from baggage claim, ridden the shuttle to the adjacent train station, deciphered the cryptic train tables and many challenging British accents, purchased my ticket from a reluctant kiosk, and arrived at the correct platform, there she is, the woman from the plane. She glances up, probably sensing my stunned stare, sees me, looks momentarily stunned herself, then looks away.

We don't make eye contact again but stand a few yards

apart on the platform, waiting for our train. I hold very still, as if it will quell the tumult inside me. I have fleeting, stupid thoughts, like maybe it is *fate* and who am I to defy the Fates? Or, maybe in a foreign country it doesn't count as violating my abstinence?

The train finally pulls up to the platform, whipping my hair around my face. We board the same car from different doors. Again, I settle four or five rows ahead of her. My body feels rubbery with exhaustion but buzzy, animated by the prospect that something is going to *happen*. I haven't felt it in so long, this familiar excitement, this nervous attention to my body and its environs. I feel, actually, as I think about it more, just a few clicks away from *anxious*.

As I count the dwindling stops until my station, my nerves increase, until they become a kind of dread, a familiar dread, as if some outside force compels me to complete the promise of this tension, just because I can. I glance back. Her face is tilted toward the window, outside of which a field and then a small pond glide by, but I see the flicker of attention to my movement and feel the hum of the invisible cord between us, its subtle electricity, though I sense that she will not be the one to act.

I know how to do this. The right kind of question to break the silence, the conversation to follow, the casual invitation to meet up later. I haven't missed many of these opportunities in the past. Especially when I was younger, I kissed a lot of strangers. In more recent years, I've collected "friends" that sat like simmering pots, maintaining the warm promise of consummation, if ever I got hungry enough. But something is different, intercepting the usual broadcast like the song of a nearby radio station, snippets of a chorus that I begin to recognize.

My excitement is more like anxiety. I am anxious because I do not want to consummate this flirtation. I want to check into my hotel in Bloomsbury and get some dinner, alone. I want to release myself from this nervous bondage. And suddenly, I realize that I can. I can give myself permission to stop. I let the cord go slack. I let it go completely.

Then, it's as if I have removed a set of headphones from my ears; the music stops and now I can hear the murmur of the other passengers in the train car, the steady rush of our motion against the tracks. My body feels hollowed out, but I'm in here—complete and alone, not casting outside myself to find some other body. Not a zombie, or a Roomba, or a heat-seeking missile. I scoot over into the seat by the window and close my eyes.

We get off at the same stop, and by now I'm neither excited nor surprised by this. I am groggy, having been lulled into half sleep for the final twenty minutes of our journey. I deboard the train a few passengers behind the woman, and watch her walk straight into the arms of another woman who is waiting for her on the platform. They embrace for a long time and as I pass them, I smile, and keep on walking toward the taxi stand, my steps heavy with relief.

I give the driver my hotel's address and lean back in my seat. I observe the buildings we pass, all of them smaller and prettier than what I'm used to in New York, and wonder why I have chosen this time to indulge my old routine. I have traveled abroad before, but I now realize that every time I was either with a lover or I found someone, was pulled through the experience by a humming cord or one that had quieted with familiarity. I am *alone* in a way I have never been. I have had to build a reference for each new kind of aloneness, and the first time is the hardest. I just didn't see this one coming.

I was so quick to try to escape the feeling of being in a foreign place without someone else to distract me. I discover that I *am* lonely, but not in an urgent or absorbing way, not the kind that obscures everything else. This loneliness is a mist that wafts through me and which I trust will pass. It feels more like a kind of sorrow than a sickness. It will return, during one of my solitary dinners, or on the listing deck of that great ship, but I won't need another body to shield me from it. Sitting with it, I recognize it as an essential aloneness, one that exists whether we stop to acknowledge it or spend our lives running from it into the arms of strangers. For all those years, I had mistaken it for a problem to be fixed, but this kind of aloneness is not the symptom of a deficit, or a loss. No matter how we grasp at other people, compare the words we find for what fills us, we are still alone with ourselves. No matter whom I loved, I was always alone with myself. By avoiding that fact, I had stayed a stranger to myself.

I pay the driver and lug my suitcase into the hotel lobby. As

I wait for the concierge behind a couple with two young children, I notice a different kind of excitement. It isn't nervous at all. I am happy to see myself, after those hours spent gone, lost in a story whose ending I no longer care to know. I am happy to be alone, even to be lonely, in this new city. I forgot, for a spell, that my own company is more compelling than that of any stranger, and returning to this knowledge feels like a kind of love, like walking straight into the arms of a friend.

About the Contributors

JEFFERY RENARD ALLEN is the author of five books, including the novels *Song of the Shank* and *Rails Under My Back*, which won the *Chicago Tribune*'s Heartland Prize for Fiction; the short story collection *Holding Pattern*, which received the Ernest J. Gaines Award for Literary Excellence; and two collections of poetry. Allen is the recipient of a Whiting Writers' Award, a grant in Innovative Literature from the Creative Capital Foundation, and a Guggenheim Fellowship. He makes his home in Johannesburg. Find out more about him at www.authorjefferyrenardallen.com.

PETER HO DAVIES is the author, most recently, of *A Lie Someone Told You About Yourself.* His other books include *The Fortunes*, winner of the Anisfield-Wolf Award, and *The Welsh Girl*, long-listed for the Man Booker Prize. His short stories have appeared in *Harper's Magazine*, *The Atlantic*, *The Paris Review*, and *Granta*, and have been anthologized in *The O. Henry Prize Stories* and *The Best American Short Stories.*

CLAIRE DEDERER is the author of the critically acclaimed memoirs *Love and Trouble* and *Poser*, which was a *New York*

Times bestseller. She is at work on *Monsters*, a book about bad people who make great art, for Knopf. The book is based on her globally viral *Paris Review* essay "What Do We Do with the Art of Monstrous Men?" Dederer has written for *The New York Times*, *The Atlantic*, *The Nation*, *Vogue*, and many other publications. She teaches in the MFA program at Pacific University and lives on an island in Puget Sound.

ANTHONY DOERR's most recent book is *Cloud Cuckoo Land*. His previous novel, *All the Light We Cannot See*, won the Pulitzer Prize, the Carnegie Medal, the Alex Award, and was a number one *New York Times* bestseller, and his short stories have appeared in *The Best American Short Stories*, *The O. Henry Prize Stories*, *New American Stories*, and *The Scribner Anthology of Contemporary Short Fiction*. Doerr lives in Boise, Idaho, with his wife and sons.

LENA DUNHAM is an award-winning writer, director, actor, and producer. Her production company, Good Thing Going, has a full slate of projects across film, television, theater, and podcasting. The creator, writer, and star of the hit HBO series *Girls*, Dunham has likewise served as writer, director, and producer on such shows as HBO and BBC's *Industry* and HBO's *Camping*. Dunham is a *New York Times* bestselling author and regular contributor to publications such as *Vogue*, *Harper's Magazine*, and *The New York Times*.

MELISSA FEBOS is the author of the memoir *Whip Smart* and two essay collections: *Abandon Me* and *Girlhood*. She is the inaugural winner of the Jeanne Córdova Nonfiction Award from Lambda Literary and the recipient of fellowships from the MacDowell Colony, Bread Loaf, Lower Manhattan Cultural Council, the BAU Institute, Vermont Studio Center, the Barbara Deming Foundation, and others, and her essays have appeared in *The Paris Review*, *The Believer*, *McSweeney's Quarterly*, *Granta*, *The Sewanee Review*, *Tin House*, *The Sun*, and *The New York Times*. She is an associate professor at the University of Iowa, where she teaches in the nonfiction writing program.

HELENA FITZGERALD is an essayist whose work has appeared online or in print in *The Atlantic*, *The Cut*, *The New Republic*, *Hazlitt*, *Marie Claire*, *Rolling Stone*, *GQ*, *The New Inquiry*, and *Catapult*, among many other publications. She also writes "Griefbacon," a long-running weekly essay-newsletter about feelings.

AJA GABEL's debut novel, *The Ensemble*, is out now from Riverhead Books. Her prose can be found in *The Cut*, *Buzzfeed*, *Kenyon Review*, *BOMB*, and elsewhere. She studied writing at Wesleyan University and the University of Virginia and has a PhD in literature and creative writing from the University of Houston. Currently she lives and writes in Los Angeles.

MEGAN GIDDINGS's first novel, *Lakewood*, was a nominee for two NAACP Image Awards and a Los Angeles Times Book Prize in the Ray Bradbury Speculative, Science Fiction, and Fantasy category. It was one of NPR's Best Books of 2020, a Michigan Notable Book for 2021, and one of *New York* magazine's 10 Best Books of 2020. She is an assistant professor at Michigan State University and affiliate faculty at Antioch University's low-residency MFA. Her second book, *The Women Could Fly*, will be published by Amistad in 2022.

LEV GROSSMAN is the author of the number one *New York Times*–bestselling *Magicians* trilogy, which has been published in twenty-five countries and adapted for television. His novel *The Silver Arrow* was one of the *Times'* best children's books of 2020, and he wrote the film *The Map of Tiny Perfect Things*, which premiered on Amazon in 2021. Grossman's journalism has appeared in *TIME*, *The New York Times*, *Vanity Fair*, *Slate*, *Wired*, *The Wall Street Journal*, and many other publications. He lives in Brooklyn with his wife and three children.

JEAN KWOK is the award-winning, *New York Times*– and internationally bestselling author of *Searching for Sylvie Lee*, *Girl in Translation*, and *Mambo in Chinatown*. Her work has been published in twenty countries and taught in universities, colleges, and high schools across the world. An instant *New York Times* bestseller, *Searching for Sylvie Lee* was selected for the Read with Jenna Today Show Book Club and featured in *The New York Times*, *Time*, *Newsweek*, the *New York Post*, *The*

Washington Post, *O*, *The Oprah Magazine*, *People*, *Entertainment Weekly*, on CNN, and more. She is trilingual, fluent in Dutch, Chinese, and English, and studied Latin for seven years. She lives in the Netherlands with her husband and two sons.

JHUMPA LAHIRI is the author of five works of fiction— *Interpreter of Maladies*, *The Namesake*, *Unaccustomed Earth*, *The Lowland*, and *Whereabouts*, and two works of nonfiction, *In Other Words*—her first book written in Italian, originally published as *In Altre Parole*—and *The Clothing of Books*, originally published in Italian as *Il Vestito dei Libri*. She's also the author of one book of poems, written in Italian as *Il quaderno di Nerina* (*Nerina's Notebook*). Lahiri has received numerous awards, including the Pulitzer Prize; the PEN/Hemingway Award; the PEN/Malamud Award; the Frank O'Connor International Short Story Award; the Premio Gregor von Rezzori; the DSC Prize for South Asian Literature; a National Humanities Medal, awarded by President Barack Obama; and the Premio Internazionale Viareggio-Versilia. She divides her time between Princeton and Rome.

YIYUN LI is the author of six works of fiction—*Must I Go*, *Where Reasons End*, *Kinder Than Solitude*, *A Thousand Years of Good Prayers*, *The Vagrants*, and *Gold Boy, Emerald Girl*—and the memoir *Dear Friend, from My Life I Write to You in Your Life*. She is the recipient of many awards, including a PEN/Hemingway Award, a PEN/Jean Stein Book Award, a MacArthur Fellowship, and a Windham-Campbell Prize, and was featured in *The New Yorker*'s 20 Under 40 fiction issue. Her work has appeared in *The New Yorker*, *A Public Space*, *Best American Short Stories*, and *The O. Henry Prize Stories*, among other publications. She teaches at Princeton University and lives in Princeton, New Jersey.

MAILE MELOY is the author of three novels, two short story collections, a middle-grade trilogy, and a picture book. Her fiction has appeared in *The New Yorker* and *The Best American Short Stories* and on *Selected Shorts* and *This American Life*. She has received *The Paris Review*'s Aga Khan Prize, the PEN/Malamud Award, the E. B. White Award, two California Book Awards, and a Guggenheim Fellowship.

DINA NAYERI is the author of *The Ungrateful Refugee*, winner of the Geschwister Scholl Preis, finalist for the Los Angeles Times Book Prize, Kirkus Prize, and *ELLE*'s Grand prix des lectrices. A 2019–2020 fellow at the Columbia Institute for Ideas and Imagination in Paris and a 2021 Fellow at the American Library in Paris, Nayeri been awarded an NEA grant in literature and UNESCO City of Literature Paul Engle Prize, and she been published in more than twenty countries and in *The New York Times*, *The New Yorker*, *The Guardian*, *Granta*, *The O. Henry Prize Stories*, *The Best American Short Stories*, and many other publications.

IMANI PERRY is the Hughes Rogers Professor of African American Studies at Princeton University. She is the author of six books, including the award-winning *Looking for Lorraine:*

The Radiant and Radical Life of Lorraine Hansberry. Her most recent book is *Breathe: A Letter to My Sons.* She lives in the Philadelphia area with her children.

EMILY RABOTEAU is the author of *The Professor's Daughter,* a novel, and *Searching for Zion,* winner of an American Book Award. She teaches creative writing at the City College of New York, CUNY. Her next book, *Caution: Lessons in Survival,* is forthcoming from Holt.

MAYA SHANBHAG LANG is the author of *What We Carry: A Memoir,* a *New York Times Book Review* Editors' Choice and Amazon Best Book of 2020. She is also the author of *The Sixteenth of June.* She holds a PhD in comparative literature and lives with her daughter just outside of New York City.

AMY SHEARN is the author of the novels *The Mermaid of Brooklyn, How Far Is the Ocean from Here,* and *Unseen City,* Gold Medal winner of the 2021 Independent Publisher Book Award for Literary Fiction. She is a senior editor at *Medium,* and her work has appeared in *The New York Times, Slate, Literary Hub,* and many other publications. Shearn has an MFA from the University of Minnesota and currently lives in Brooklyn with her two children.

MAGGIE SHIPSTEAD is the *New York Times*–bestselling author of the novels *Great Circle, Astonish Me,* and *Seating Arrangements,* which was the winner of the Dylan Thomas Prize and the Los Angeles Times Book Prize for First Fiction. She is a graduate of the Iowa Writers' Workshop, a former Wallace Stegner Fellow at Stanford, and the recipient of a fellowship from the National Endowment for the Arts.

JESMYN WARD received her MFA from the University of Michigan and has received a MacArthur Fellowship, a Wallace Stegner Fellowship, a John and Renee Grisham Writers Residency, and the Strauss Living Prize. She is the winner of two National Book Awards for Fiction for *Sing, Unburied, Sing* (2017) and *Salvage the Bones* (2011). She is also the author of the novel *Where the Line Bleeds*, the illustrated speech *Navigate Your Stars*, and the memoir *Men We Reaped*, a recipient of numerous awards. Ward is currently a professor of creative writing at Tulane University and lives in Mississippi.

LIDIA YUKNAVITCH is the author of the bestselling novels *The Book of Joan* (Harper Books), *The Small Backs of Children* (Harper Books), and *Dora: A Headcase* (Hawthorne Books), as well as an anti-memoir, *The Chronology of Water* (Hawthorne Books), adapted for film by Kristen Stewart, and *The Misfit's Manifesto*, based on her TED Talk "On the Beauty of Being a Misfit" (now with over 3.5 million views). She has a PhD in literature from the University of Oregon, and is the founder of the non-academic creative lab Corporeal Writing in Portland, Oregon. Her short story collection *Verge* (Riverhead) came out in paperback in 2021, and her novel *Thrust* is forthcoming from Riverhead in 2022. She is a very good swimmer.

Acknowledgments

Heartfelt thanks to my wonderful agent, Jody Kahn, for her dedication, patience, and friendship; my editor, Leigh Newman, for her unwavering belief and keen eye; my publisher, Andy Hunter; and the entire dream team at Catapult, especially Wah-Ming Chang and Alisha Gorder, for welcoming this book and helping it fly.

To Edith Zimmerman, whose friendship I cherish and whose wildly supportive emails are my version of Medici patronage. To beloveds near and far: Lauren DeMille, Annie Kwon, Ashlie Hubbard, Erin Weckerle, Ilana Lapid. To my family, especially my parents, Bonnie and Ted Garrett, and my brother, Brandon Louis Garrett.

To my wise and generous contributors: Thank you for saying yes, for trusting me with your vulnerable stories, and for collaborating during our long collective isolation and making it less lonely. Your words have infused *The Lonely Stories* with a kind of magic. I'm deeply grateful.

To my children, Serafina and Aurelio: Thank you for the tightest hugs and deepest laughs, and for being a source of light even in dark times. I love you forever.

And finally, thank you to Tony, for everything.

Permissions

ABOUT THE EDITOR

NATALIE EVE GARRETT is an artist and writer. She's the editor of *Eat Joy: Stories & Comfort Food from 31 Celebrated Writers*, a collection of personal stories with recipes exploring how food can help us cope in dark times. She is also the editor of *The Artists' and Writers' Cookbook: A Collection of Stories with Recipes* (powerHouse Books, 2016). A graduate of Yale University with an MFA in painting from the University of Pennsylvania, Garrett lives with her husband, daughter, and son in a town outside D.C., along the Potomac River.